Raising an ADHD Child

of related interest

The Parents' Guide to ADHD Medicines
Professor Peter Hill
ISBN 978 1 78775 568 0
eISBN 978 1 78775 569 7

Step by Step Help for Children with ADHD
A Self-Help Manual for Parents
Anne Weeks, Cathy Laver-Bradbury, David Daley, Edmund
J. S. Sonuga-Barke and Margaret Thompson
ISBN 978 1 84905 070 8
eISBN 978 0 85700 235 8

Parenting Rewired
How to Raise a Happy Autistic Child in a Very Neurotypical World
Danielle Punter and Charlotte Chaney
ISBN 978 1 83997 072 6
eISBN 978 1 83997 073 3

Parenting Dual Exceptional Children
Supporting a Child Who Has High Learning Potential and
Special Educational Needs and Disabilities
Denise Yates
Illustrated by Paul Pickford
Forewords by Lydia Niomi Christie and Sal McKeown
ISBN 978 1 78775 810 0
eISBN 978 1 78775 811 7

Raising an ADHD Child

A Handbook for Parents for Distractible, Dreamy and Defiant Children

Fintan O'Regan and **Zoe Beezer**

Illustrated by Richard Johnston

Jessica Kingsley Publishers
London and Philadelphia

First published in Great Britain in 2024 by Jessica Kingsley Publishers
An imprint of John Murray Press

2

Copyright © Fintan O'Regan and Zoe Beezer 2024
Illustration Copyright © Richard Johnston 2024

The right of Fintan O'Regan and Zoe Beezer to be identified as the Author of the Work has
been asserted by them in accordance with the Copyright, Designs and Patents Act 1988.

Disclaimer: The information contained in this book is not intended to replace the
services of trained medical professionals or to be a substitute for medical advice.
You are advised to consult a doctor on any matters relating to your health, and in
particular on any matters that may require diagnosis or medical attention.

A CIP catalogue record for this title is available from the
British Library and the Library of Congress

ISBN 978 1 83997 021 4
eISBN 978 1 83997 022 1

Printed and bound by CPI Group (UK) Ltd, Croydon, CR0 4YY

Jessica Kingsley Publishers' policy is to use papers that are natural, renewable and recyclable
products and made from wood grown in sustainable forests. The logging and manufacturing
processes are expected to conform to the environmental regulations of the country of origin.

Jessica Kingsley Publishers
Carmelite House
50 Victoria Embankment
London EC4Y 0DZ

www.jkp.com

John Murray Press
Part of Hodder & Stoughton Limited
An Hachette UK Company

Contents

Preface from Fin and Zoe

Being a parent of a child, as they say, does not come with a manual, but will be a journey of finding out about your child and also finding out about yourself.

All children are unique and different, however there are some children who may appear to be out of step with some of the traditional developmental stages of their peers. This group can include children with ADHD. As a result, we have written this book to support parents of children and teenagers with ADHD.

Our focus will be initially on demystifying ADHD and providing a greater understanding of the developmental differences in these children, as well as providing a number of systems and strategies for support.

As a former headteacher of a specialist school and a parent myself I can confirm that the journey of raising children to maximise their potential can be filled with twists and turns along the way. We hope that the many suggestions from both research and decades of experience in the field will help you on this journey.

Fin

Writing this book has taken me on a bit of a voyage of discovery – just as I hope it will do for you. Before putting pen to paper, I was a parent to both neurodivergent and neurotypical children, I had been an assistant head of inclusion and wellbeing and had accrued many years of experience running special needs departments in a variety of schools, and I thought I had a reasonable understanding of my universe, both personal and professional. However, this book has allowed me to research deeper into the nuances and subtleties of the wonderful world of ADHD, and it has helped me to understand how to parent my ADHD children (and non-ADHD children) better – inevitably I still do not get it right all of the time, but I am trying to learn to be kinder to myself, and less self-critical when this happens, because, as Fin says, parenting does not come with a manual. This book has also helped me to have a greater insight into the overlap of neurodivergent conditions, which I try to hold in mind when I assess young people; in addition, it has led to more effective conversations with parents, school leaders, teachers, and governors, about how to provide better 'whole-person' support for children and teenagers with ADHD. Along the way, my research has also caused me to self-reflect about my own personality and to recognise certain traits and characteristics in myself, in a way I had not done before.

My hope for this book is that it will help you to understand your child better, and it will give you tips and tricks to handle the tricky situations that crop up all the time when parenting. I hope it also helps you to deal with external agencies, such as assessors and educational establishments, and encourages you to create positive working relationships with the professionals involved in your child's life, so that you can all work together to support your child. It may, like it did for me, also trigger some self-reflection along the way, and enable you to recognise some of the characteristics that you see in your child within yourself (in adult form). Whether this last point resonates or not, hopefully you will be able to dip in and out of this book as your child reaches different milestones, or when you need help to get back on track in times of need or uncertainty!

Zoe

An explanation of terms

- We have used the word 'neurotypical' (for people who do not have ADHD) and 'neurodivergent' (for people who have ADHD and other co-occurring conditions), although we appreciate that terms are constantly being reviewed and improved.
- We have referred to children and teenagers in this book as people 'with ADHD' and 'ADHD children/teenagers', interchangeably.

An explanation about chapters

As you read through this book you will detect the voice of the two different authors, so we thought it would be helpful if we identified which chapters each of us took the lead on; however all of the information outlined is a combination and a culmination of our joint philosophy, experience and expertise in this journey of supporting children and young persons with ADHD.

Chapter	Author
1 lead	Fin
2 lead	Zoe
3 lead	Zoe
4 lead	Fin
5 lead	Zoe
6 lead	Fin
7 lead	Fin
8 lead	Zoe
9 lead	Zoe
10 lead	Fin
Appendices	Both

Disclaimer: The information contained in this book is not intended to replace the services of trained medical professionals or to be a substitute for medical advice. You are advised to consult a doctor on any matters relating to your health, and in particular on any matters that may require diagnosis or medical attention.

Chapter 1

EXPLANATION AND NOT AN EXCUSE

Understanding and supporting your child with ADHD

In this chapter we will:

- demystify the term ADHD and consider the key symptoms
- take a look at a brief history of what we today call ADHD
- investigate a new way of looking at the condition.

ADHD demystified

Some years ago I was asked to speak to a parent support group meeting on ASD issues, as I was at that time the head of a specialist school in South London, when I heard two parents talking.

I overheard one parent saying to the other, 'The doctor says that my son doesn't have ASD, he has ADD.' 'What's that?' said the second parent.

The first parent replied, 'I'm not exactly sure, I think it stands for attention devastation disorder.'

Though at the time I may have initially smiled at the mistake, I thought that actually that might well describe the impact that her son was having on the family – and that is no laughing matter.

The symptoms of ADHD in children and teenagers are well defined, and they're usually noticeable before the age of 6. They occur in more than one situation, such as at home and at school.

Children may have symptoms of both inattentiveness and hyperactivity and impulsiveness, or they may have symptoms of just one of these types of behaviour.

Inattentiveness (difficulty concentrating and focusing):
The main signs of inattentiveness are:

- having a short attention span and being easily distracted
- making careless mistakes – for example, in schoolwork
- appearing forgetful or losing things
- being unable to stick to tasks that are tedious or time-consuming
- appearing to be unable to listen to or carry out instructions
- constantly changing activity or task
- having difficulty organising tasks.

Hyperactivity and impulsiveness:
The main signs of hyperactivity and impulsiveness are:

- being unable to sit still, especially in calm or quiet surroundings
- constantly fidgeting
- being unable to concentrate on tasks
- excessive physical movement
- excessive talking
- being unable to wait their turn
- acting without thinking
- interrupting conversations
- little or no sense of danger.

(NHS, 2021)

These symptoms can cause significant problems in a child's life, such as underachievement at school, poor social interaction with other children and adults, and problems with discipline.

This book will be outlining ways and means of understanding the condition and how to support children who have it. Let's start by considering the 'triad' of core features which are as follows:

1. Poor attention span
2. Excessive impulsivity
3. Hyperactivity.

(APA, 2013)

Symptoms of attention may include being disorganised, forgetful, easily distracted and finding it difficult to sustain attention in tasks or play activities, while hyperactive or impulsive behaviours may include fidgeting, having trouble playing quietly, interrupting others and always being on the go. While such behaviours exist in all of us from time to time, the difference is the degree and intensity in individuals with ADHD.

Though academic and behavioural issues within the school programme appear high on the agenda, a main area of concern in children with attention issues will be the issue of socialisation or interaction with other children. Often individuals with traits of ADHD can appear quite amusing within a group of peers, but this 'class clown' effect soon wears thin to be replaced by impatience and intolerance of the constant interruptions that often take place. This can lead to isolation of the individual from the peer group.

In addition, many problems for children with traits of ADHD stem from their inability to handle the various degrees of environmental stimuli that come their way. This is why they operate best in a consistent structure providing them with safety and security to stay on task.

ADHD occurs in approximately 3–9 per cent of school-age children, and is roughly three times more likely to be diagnosed in males than in females. ADHD develops in childhood, often by 3–5 years of age, and research suggests that 80 per cent of children diagnosed in childhood continue to be impaired by the condition in adolescence, and that up to 67 per cent continue to have symptoms producing impairment into adulthood.

As noted above, lack of focus, poor control, impulsivity, inappropriate behaviours and distractibility are often hallmarks of children who are diagnosed with ADHD. The symptoms, however, are not necessarily seen to the same degree in all children who are diagnosed. As a result, clinicians recognise three subtypes of the disorder: ADHD predominantly hyperactive-impulsive type; ADHD predominantly inattentive type (sometimes referred to as ADD); and ADHD combined type, which describes the majority of cases.

A brief history

The starting point of ADHD as we know it today is generally seen as being in lectures given in 1902 by the English paediatrician Sir George Still (1968–1941) who described 'an abnormal defect of moral control in children' and found that some affected children, while intelligent, could not control their behaviour in the way a typical child would (Still, 1902). It is not without irony that a man called Still was talking about individuals who were not.

In 1937, the German physicians Franz Kramer (1878–1967) and Hans Pollnow (1902–1943) described 'a hyperkinetic disease of infancy'. They noted an urgent character to the motor activity of affected children, who could not stay still, liked to run and climb, and were unhappy when prevented from doing so (Kramer and Pollnow, 1932).

Around the same time as Kramer and Pollnow's work, the American psychiatrist Charles Bradley (1902–1979) administered benzedrine sulphate, an amphetamine that had recently been approved for medical use in the USA, to ease headaches in a children's home in Rhode Island. He discovered that, unexpectedly, his young patients' behaviour and performance in school improved as a side effect of the medicine (Bradley, 1937); however his findings were largely ignored and it was not until many years later that doctors and researchers began to recognise the importance of his discovery. Eventually, this work led to the development of medications such as Ritalin, widely used to manage ADHD today.

ADHD in its present form is largely a result of reclassification of key traits over a period of time.

Having initially been regarded as term used to describe hyperactivity, the American Psychiatric Association's *Diagnostic and Statistical Manual of Mental Disorders* (commonly known to professionals as the 'DSM') is credited with its current diagnostic status.

The DSM is a publication that lists all the recognised mental health disorders along with their causes, risk factors and treatments, and although ADHD was not listed in the first edition (the DSM-1) in 1952, the second edition in 1968 included 'hyperkinetic impulse disorder' for the first time.

The third edition in 1980 changed the name to 'attention deficit disorder' (ADD) and finally this was revised in 1987 to 'attention deficit hyperactivity disorder' (ADHD). However the condition was still poorly understood and under-researched, and it was not until the DSM's fourth and fifth editions of 1994 and 2013 that the description of ADHD came to resemble the condition we recognise today.

A new way of thinking about ADHD

So often when we consider the term ADHD we think of it as a problem or as a challenge. Indeed the 'D' of 'devastation' in the story earlier could be replaced with terms such as 'disruptive', 'distractible', 'dreamy' or even 'defiant'.

Part of this I think is this because the 'attention' and 'hyperactivity' traits in the term are surrounded by the Ds of 'deficit' and 'disorder' which does tend to frame the term as a negative.

So the question is, is it helpful to consider ADHD as a deficit or even a disorder in terms of supporting individuals, both as children and as adults?

It is often true that individuals with ADHD can struggle in adjusting to age-related expectations in comparison to their peers. In Chapter 2 when we introduce and discuss the term 'executive function' we shall outline that ADHD often affects the outcomes of processing and control of thoughts, actions and emotions.

It should also be pointed out that individuals with ADHD often have traits of creativity, energy and spontaneity, which in certain situations could be viewed as benefits or actually advantages over peers.

The letter 'D' also stands for two other truly important terms with respect to ADHD: 'developmental' and 'difference'. This is because ADHD is a term that describes neurodevelopmental differences in children, adolescents and adults, and the more that we are able to understand the traits of the condition, the more effective are the systems and strategies that can be deployed for support.

I prefer therefore to see ADHD not as a challenge but rather an opportunity, and not as a disorder, but as individuals who may respond 'differently' in the some of the ways they learn, behave and interact with others.

As a result I propose to reconsider the negative 'Ds' in the term ADHD and replace them with more practical and accurate 'Ds': 'attention developmental hyperactivity difference'.

In order to best to support individuals who are 'developmentally different', let us outline some of the areas in this book that we will be covering in terms of practical and proactive support by sharing a short anecdote with you.

Some years ago I attended a conference which was called Teaching the Brain. A colleague called out and said 'I don't teach brains, I teach students' – whilst a few people laughed I was instantly struck by the thought that the delegate was right. We don't teach brains – we should focus on individuals and on their minds.

So what is the difference between the brain and the mind? The brain is an organ and a vessel in which the electronic impulses that create thought are contained. With the brain you coordinate your moves, your activities and transmit impulses. But you use the mind to think. You can muse at what has happened, what is scheduled and what might happen.

I recently came across an article by the Australian neuroscientist Jared Cooney Horvath called 'Change your mind about the brain' (2016). He suggested that most of the research around learning tends to centre on what is happening in the brain. He also points out that 'Teachers don't teach brains – they teach minds.'

The mind is the promoter of thought, perception, emotion, determination, memory and imagination that takes place within the brain. The mind is often used to refer to the thought processes of reason, the awareness of consciousness and the ability to control what we do and know what we are doing. In essence, the ability to understand.

We know that animals can interpret their environments but may not be able to understand them. Humans appear better able to understand what happens around them and therefore adapt accordingly – although there may be individuals you have come across who cause you to disagree with that statement.

The mind vs brain debate has been going on at least since the time of Aristotle. He and Plato argued that the soul housed intelligence or wisdom and that it could not be placed within the physical body. Rene Descartes, the 17th-century French philosopher, identified the mind with consciousness and self-awareness, with an ability to distinguish itself from the brain. However, he still called the brain the seat of intelligence.

Regardless of whether the mind is contained in the brain or exists beyond these physical boundaries, it is evident that it is something immense. The question is how we should maximise its potential.

Horvarth advocates that the key is to involve or engage not just the brain in learning, but also the body and the environment. We need to make sure that both of these are included in planning the approach to support individuals with ADHD.

To effectively support individuals with ADHD you should consider not just supporting their mind but their body and the environment.

ADHD in adults

It is also worth making the point that ADHD is not just a childhood condition affecting boys and girls, but will also affect individuals into adulthood. Specialists within the NHS have suggested the following as a list of symptoms associated with ADHD in adults:

- Carelessness and lack of attention to detail
- Continually starting new tasks before finishing old ones
- Poor organisational skills
- Inability to focus or prioritise
- Continually losing or misplacing things
- Forgetfulness
- Restlessness and edginess
- Difficulty keeping quiet, and speaking out of turn
- Blurting out responses and often interrupting others
- Mood swings, irritability and a quick temper
- Inability to deal with stress
- Extreme impatience
- Taking risks in activities, often with little or no regard for personal safety or the safety of others – for example, driving dangerously.

(NHS, 2021)

This does mean of course that symptoms persist over the years. ADHD cannot be cured, but individuals grow with it rather than growing out of it.

What this means in essence is that individuals with ADHD will continue to need support in areas where they may lack the skills of impulse control and concentration due to their developmental differences. However, we also need to consider the strengths they have in a host of other areas which may provide advantages as they progress through life. Within a number of publications these days explaining adult symptoms of ADHD the talk is of advantages and not disadvantages – for example, an article by the Attention Deficit Disorder Association (n.d.) lays out five positive attributes of ADHD as an adult in the job market.

Creativity. People with ADHD can be some of the most creative resources on a team, bringing energy and new approaches to their projects. Several studies have shown that adults with ADHD tend to be out-of-the-box thinkers.

Hyper-focus, quality and timeliness. When focused on work that aligns with their interests and strengths, individuals with ADHD frequently draw upon their strength of hyper-focus and deliver results. Organisations can create a competitive advantage by capitalising on the diversity ADHD minds bring to their teams.

Good in crises. A recent study also found that the ADHD brain can make individuals great in a crisis. We often see higher rates of ADHD among A&E doctors and nurses, police officers, fire and rescue personnel, journalists, stock traders, professional athletes and entertainers. When others are in crisis, those with ADHD can be cool, calm and under control.

Intuitive and detailed-oriented. Individuals with ADHD seem to notice things others miss, sometimes to the point of seeming extraordinarily intuitive. The average brain manages to sort and filter all incoming sights, sounds, tastes, smells and touch sensations to a manageable 40 bits of information per second. The ADHD brain is overloaded with sensory input and faces issues with executive function – sorting, filtering, discarding, prioritising, following through, tracking progress and following procedures. However, since the ADHD brain lets in a lot of what some employees might consider irrelevant noise, sometimes they are able to notice things that others naturally filter out.

Quick starters. While impulsivity is an ADHD symptom, that often means that people with ADHD are quick starters. They jump right in without worrying or doing endless research. If your team is resistant to risk, resistant to change, hung up on process and procedure, you know it can take forever to get anything done. People resist change and will stick with systems even if they don't work, or get stuck in analysis paralysis. Although sometimes employees with ADHD struggle to get started, often once they do get going on something that they're passionate about, they are able to hyper-focus!

(Attention Deficit Disorder Association, n.d.)

One final note in this opening chapter is to repeat that while the letter 'D' starts the words 'deficit' and 'disorder', it also stands for 'developmental' and 'difference', as well as 'diagnosis', 'determination', 'desire' and 'destiny'. So let's focus on the positive 'Ds' to help and support individuals with ADHD.

KEY POINTS

- ADHD is a condition that has not only recently come about due to the advent of computers or changes in diet; we are just using a term that describes a number of symptoms, behaviours or traits that have existed in individuals throughout history.
- Although the term itself has undergone changes in description, the key traits of hyperactivity/hypoactivity, impulsivity and inattention are consistently included within the spectrum of the term.
- The stigma of ADHD as a problem condition thankfully is gradually being removed. What would help this process further would be the reset and hopefully removal of the terms 'deficit' and 'disorder', which are misleading and not accurate, and replacing them with the terms 'developmental' and 'difference' within the ADHD label.
- Whilst ADHD can provide a challenge for individuals affected it can also provide an opportunity in how to react and think differently. Especially in adulthood it is being reframed in a much more positive way.

AND ALSO...

ADHD is not something that has emerged as a result of modern society or as a result of technology in an ever changing world. There have always been individuals with traits of hyperactivity, impulsivity and inattention throughout history. The term itself is an attempt to understand developmental differences in children and adults, and more importantly to support all individuals to fulfil their potential.

Chapter 2

DIAGNOSIS AND CO-OCCURRENCE

Understanding how and when to consider diagnosis, and whether your child has any overlapping conditions

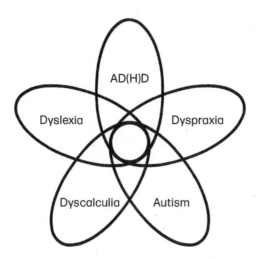

In this chapter we will signpost:

- things to consider before a diagnosis
- when and how to consider a formal diagnosis, and what to look out for
- how to effectively identify and support traits and characteristics both at school and at home, pending any diagnosis
- overlapping traits and characteristics in respect of the most common co-occurring conditions.

Things to consider before a diagnosis

I have personal experience of pursuing an ADHD diagnosis for two of my four children, and in my professional life I have helped multiple pupils (and their parents) through the diagnostic process.

The routes to my own children's diagnoses were very different from each other. The first took me by surprise! My daughter was 18 at the time and had a pre-existing diagnosis of autism spectrum condition (ASC; also known as Asperger's syndrome) – what I wasn't expecting was that ADHD would also come into the mix! However, when I reflect on my parenting of her over those preceding 18 years, I can see in retrospect that I was confusing some ADHD traits with ASC characteristics. A typical girl, my daughter had developed coping strategies to hide and to support some of her weaker executive function skills (discussed in Chapter 3); as a result, it took me and her school longer to realise that as the curriculum became harder, requiring greater sustained academic application to access it, that impulsivity and inattention were affecting her progress – and so at the age of 18 her self-help strategies and her desire to mask and internalise her symptoms were no longer sophisticated enough to conceal her ADHD traits, and she became distractible and dreamy in class.

My son on the other hand received a diagnosis at the age of 13 – and to be honest he had been displaying traits at home for many years. I had therefore been waiting for school to catch up and see what we were witnessing. Then in Year 9, the landscape changed, and my son's desire for increased independence and his resistance to the support that I had been giving him up to that point meant that certain characteristics were suddenly visible in school – his poor executive function skills meant he went to school without essential equipment, forgot to bring things home, and became more distracting and distractible in class – and, from the school's point of view, he probably became more irritating. Of course, teachers started to report this to us, and thus started his assessment process.

I think these two personal accounts highlight some of the key issues that we, as parents, face:

- Frequently there are co-occurring differences and difficulties which can make the steps to diagnosis more complicated, and more confusing. It is said that 75 per cent of people with ADHD have co-occurring conditions.

- Before pursing an ADHD diagnosis, the ADHD traits need to be apparent in two different settings – this is usually school and home. When they *are* observed in both settings steps can be taken to investigate and formalise what might be going on.
- There is a 3:1 ratio of boys to girls who are diagnosed with ADHD – meaning that a lot of girls are probably going undetected (as opposed to it being a condition that is more likely to affect boys). Typically, girls try to internalise and mask symptoms to conform to classroom settings, whereas boys seem to be less driven to conformity and are more likely to overtly display the factors which interrupt their learning.
- One explanation of ADHD is that it is an impairment of the brain's management system, known as its executive function – sometimes described as the air traffic control system of the brain – which affects problems with attention, motivation and planning. Poor executive function skills manifest themselves in a chaotic lifestyle, forgetfulness and difficulty sustaining attention – to name a few examples. This is explored more fully in Chapter 3.

In addressing the issues within this chapter, I am in the fairly unique position of having been the SENDCo (Special Educational Needs and Disabilities Co-ordinator) at my daughter's school for most of her education, and also the SENDCo overseeing my son's progress for some of his education too. I have therefore been able to observe how and when to pursue a diagnosis from two different perspectives: as an educational professional within the same setting as my children, and as a parent, receiving feedback from teachers.

As we know from Chapter 1, the 'triad' of core ADHD features are:

1. Poor attention span
2. Excessive impulsivity
3. Hyperactivity.

(APA, 2013)

However, there are many 'hidden' or less obvious traits of ADHD, some of which are represented here:

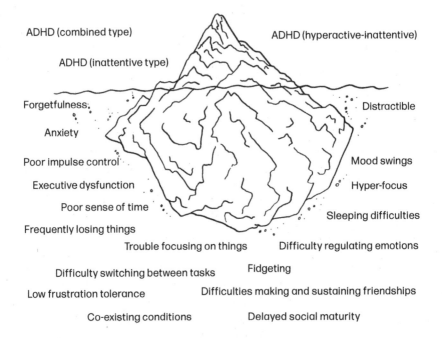

ADHD (combined type)

ADHD (hyperactive-inattentive)

ADHD (inattentive type)

Forgetfulness

Distractible

Anxiety

Poor impulse control

Mood swings

Executive dysfunction

Hyper-focus

Poor sense of time

Sleeping difficulties

Frequently losing things

Trouble focusing on things   Difficulty regulating emotions

Difficulty switching between tasks   Fidgeting

Low frustration tolerance   Difficulties making and sustaining friendships

Co-existing conditions   Delayed social maturity

A word on the 'typical' ADHD child

When considering whether your child exhibits some of the behaviours and traits associated with ADHD, it is important to point out that there is no 'typical ADHD child', and no fixed display of symptoms – the way a child's inattentiveness, impulsivity or hyperactivity manifests itself will vary from individual to individual, between boys and girls, and depending on their age and stage of development. Perhaps the one thing that all children with ADHD can be characterised by is their 'consistent inconsistency'. Of all the children that I have referred for an assessment, be that my own or those at school, no two children have been the same.

A word on hyper-focus

Whilst inattention is a core feature of ADHD, individuals with ADHD also have the ability to hyper-focus – that is the ability to focus intently on something that interests them. This includes being able to hyper-focus on technology, such as gaming and social media. The ability to hyper-focus can sometimes confuse us as parents, because there can be a misconception that ADHD is an inability to sustain attention *on anything*.

In my role as SENDCo, a very common refrain that I have heard from parents when discussing their child's classroom behaviours is: 'But he can't have ADHD because he plays his computer games for hours.' This ability to hyper-focus and lose sense of the passage of time, and perhaps fail to prioritise more important tasks, is explored in more detail in Chapter 8. Because hyper-focus is often a little-known feature of ADHD, the ability for intense focus can often cause parents to dismiss other ADHD-type characteristics and thus throw them off the scent.

A word on the meaning of 'hyperactivity'

A misunderstanding of what 'hyperactivity' means, within the context of ADHD, can also throw us parents off the scent in terms of identifying one of the key characteristics.

I have heard many parents describe their child as 'active but not hyper-active' – their impression of hyperactivity may well be that stereotypical image of the little boy hurling himself around a classroom, seemingly out of control. Hyperactivity however can be, and often is, far more subtle than that – it can be as discrete as a sense of restlessness (that often girls will try to internalise), and may be identifiable by far less obvious acts of activity than that stereotypical image – a constant movement of a leg, or fidgeting with hands or feet, a sense of energy or restlessness, or difficulty sitting still. All these markers of hyperactivity can be discrete depending on the child and their age and stage, and their sense of self-awareness.

A word on ADHD and the difference between girls and boys

It is still the case that more boys than girls are diagnosed with ADHD (as many as 3:1) but this is probably not representative of reality – what is probably more accurate is that historically girls have remained undetected. Although somewhat of a generalisation, girls tend to internalise (or hide) their symptoms and may appear dreamy in class, whereas boys tend to have more externalising features of the condition, being less self-con-scious about displaying their symptoms. Girls are therefore often easier to miss. It seems to be more accepted/expected for a girl to be 'dreamy' than a boy, meaning that teachers historically have not flagged concerns. Also, an active girl will often be passed off as a 'tomboy', whereas she may in fact be displaying traits of hyperactivity.

Teaching professionals and clinicians are becoming increasingly aware that these stereotypes need to be challenged.

The changing presentations of ADHD

The categorisation of ADHD is constantly evolving and adapting to reflect an increasing understanding of the condition. Previously children were labelled as 'ADHD' (which has the hyperactivity aspect attached to it) or 'ADD' (which is an attention deficit without the hyperactivity). The DSM-4 introduced 'subtypes' (APA, 1994), so that children were diagnosed with ADHD, but had a 'subtype' of *attention deficit* or *hyperactivity and impulsiveness* or the combined type of *attention and hyperactivity deficit*. The DSM-5 has replaced 'subtypes' with 'presentations' of ADHD (APA, 2013). This represents quite a significant change in our understanding of ADHD, because the DSM-5 now acknowledges that as a person with ADHD progresses through life and matures, the way their ADHD manifests or presents itself can also change – someone who was both hyperactive and inattentive as a child may have learnt to self-regulate their hyperactivity as an adult, and therefore the 'presentation' of their ADHD will be different in adulthood.

Changing presentations of ADHD		
Childhood	**Can change to**	**Adulthood**
Inattention Distracted and dreamy in lessons	⇨ Child learns to self-regulate as they mature	**Levels of inattention persist** Difficulty finishing tasks can persist Difficulty sustaining attention can persist
Hyperactivity Climbing, running, jumping, constantly moving	⇨ Child learns to self-regulate as they mature	**External hyperactivity traits become more discrete movements** Fidgety, a sense of impatience or restlessness
Impulsivity Behavioural disinhibition	⇨ Child learns to self-regulate as they mature	**Levels of impulsivity persist** Less overt and more often linked to verbal impulsivity – blurting things out, intruding on and interrupting conversations

When and how to pursue a formal assessment, and what to look out for

Having identified some of the things to consider before seeking a diagnosis, the next issue to consider is how to take the next steps towards getting an assessment.

When seeking an assessment, it is important to be aware of the criteria that will need to be met for a diagnosis to be considered:

- There needs to be a significant impairment in aspects of your child's social, academic or occupational functioning.
- This impairment needs to be observed in at least two different settings – usually home and school. Referring to the example I gave about my son – at home, the traits were quite obvious (an inability to remain seated during mealtimes, needing to 'fidget' when watching a film, difficulty 'switching off' and falling asleep, poor organisational skills and forgetfulness). At school, because of the structures and systems in place to help him, the traits were not obvious until there was an increased expectation for self-sufficiency within the classroom, which coincided with his own desire for greater independence.
- The clinician who carries out the assessment will want confirmation that the symptoms have been present for more than six months and are inconsistent with your child's level of development.
- In discussion with you, the assessor will wish to establish that some of the traits have been present before the age of 7 (or for those aged 17 or older, before the age of 12), and they cannot be better explained by another learning or developmental difference.
- The clinician must also be able to confirm that they are satisfied that symptoms are present before they can proceed to the diagnosis stage.

Diagnosis

Many parents choose to go down an NHS route – reporting initially to their GP and then being referred on to the appropriate specialist(s). This can sometime prove to be a battle and there is often a long wait of months before an assessment opportunity arises; this can be a draining and frustrating experience.

Therefore, many parents choose to pay for private consultations, which speeds up the process but can be quite costly.

When seeking a private assessment, be careful to choose the right professional, and where possible, ask your child's school or local ADHD support network groups for recommendations.

The professionals who can diagnose and treat ADHD are:

- paediatricians who specialise in children's health
- specialist child psychiatrists
- appropriately qualified healthcare professionals who have the correct level of training and expertise in the diagnosis of ADHD.

Because ADHD is a complex neurobiological condition, and because medication can be prescribed to try to address some of the difficulties, it is important that an assessment is conducted by a recognised professional who will be rigorous in their approach.

As part of the diagnostic process, you should expect the professional to:

- ask for feedback from school (often by completing a form called Conner's Rating Scale)
- ask for feedback from you, the parent (often by completing a parent version of the same form)
- depending on the age of your child, seek feedback from them too (often by completing the Conner's Self-Evaluation form)
- interview you and your child
- carry out a medical evaluation
- ask your child to complete a computerised assessment
- they may also do further evaluations in the form of achievement testing and intellectual testing.

The three presentations of ADHD

If your child receives a diagnosis of ADHD, the clinician will state which one of the three possible presentations they have. The descriptions and symptoms for each of the presentations are outlined in the following sections.

ADHD (inattentive presentation)

A child with this presentation will typically have higher levels of inattention and lower levels of impulsivity and hyperactivity. Historically this was thought to affect mainly girls – think of your typical daydreamer, often in her own world.

In order to hit the diagnostic criteria for an **inattentive presentation** the child needs to be affected by six or more of these nine symptoms listed below (adolescents and adults need five):

ADHD (inattentive presentation)	
Symptoms	**Examples**
Failure to pay close attention to details and makes careless mistakes	• Schoolwork is untidy or has lots of errors • Rushes through tasks
Failure to sustain attention	• Difficulty staying focused in lessons, or when reading for prolonged periods
Doesn't seem to listen	• Not listening when being spoken to directly • Needs instructions and questions repeated • Being quiet/not a 'main player' in a group setting
Difficulty following through and completing tasks	• Incomplete homework or classwork • A 'busy' brain/lots of thoughts, but a lack of motivation to act on them • Procrastination
Difficulty with organisation – and time management	• Doesn't remember to take all necessary 'kit' to school – pens etc. • Is late for things/has poor concept of the passage of time
Avoids or dislikes tasks which require sustained attention	• Difficulty with focus and application for tasks which hold little interest for them
Easily distracted	• Being distracted inside their own head • Distracted by external events – e.g. someone walking past a classroom window may take their attention away from important class announcements/learning
Often forgetful in daily activities	• Forgets to do things – such as daily chores or routines
Constantly losing things	• Disorganised with personal possessions

The inattentive type is most responsible for:

- executive function difficulties
- underachievement in school and exams
- difficulty with social functions – for example being shy and passive in social situations.

Children with this presentation can be shy and quiet in school and can often be overlooked.

ADHD (hyperactive-impulsive presentation)

A child with this presentation will typically have a difficulty with impulsivity and inattention but will have fewer issues with inattention. Traditionally this was thought to affect mainly boys – think of your typical boy who is noisy with far too much energy and unable to sit still.

In order to hit the diagnostic criteria for a **hyperactive-impulsive presentation** the child needs to be affected by six or more of these nine symptoms listed below (adolescents and adults need five):

ADHD (hyperactive-impulsive presentation)	
Symptoms	**Examples**
Fidgets with hands or feet	• Constantly moving – even in a small way such as discreetly swinging a leg
Leaves seat in class or other situations	• Difficulty sitting still
Running about or climbing excessively – or feeling of restlessness or desire to move if adult	• Climbing, running, fighting • Getting scrapes and grazes
Difficulty playing or engaging in activities quietly	• Loud • Sometimes argumentative
Often on the go or active	• Cannot sit still • Constantly moving
Blurting out answers	• Unable to hold ideas/answers in
Difficulty taking turns	• Lack of patience • Inability to wait
Interrupting	• Speaking before thinking • Unable to hold back/read a social situation before speaking
Intruding on others	• Loud, domineering • Invading personal space

It is interesting to note that the first three symptoms and the fifth ('often on the go') address hyperactivity, however most of symptoms described here are linked to impulsivity. There can be a misconception for both parents and teachers that the hallmark of ADHD is hyperactivity, and if the child does not display hyperactive traits that they cannot have ADHD. Hopefully this chapter helps to dispel that myth.

It is worth observing that compared to the inattentive presentation, the hyperactivity and impulsivity presentation has more impact in social situations because individuals often act without thinking.

ADHD (combined presentation)

This is a mix of both of the previous presentations already described. Typically, a child will present with elevated levels of inattention and hyperactive-impulsive traits.

In order to hit the diagnostic criteria for a **combined presentation**, six or more symptoms must be present in **both** the inattentive and hyperactive-impulsive presentations already described above (adolescents and adults need five in each).

How to effectively identify and support traits and characteristics both at school and at home, pending any diagnosis

Diagnosing ADHD can take time, however even in the absence of a formal diagnosis there are a number of strategies that can be adopted both at home and at school that can help to address some of the traits and challenges that your child might be experiencing.

The likelihood is that, if you are awaiting an assessment, you have already liaised with your child's school, and both you and they can see some of the characteristics of the condition. Therefore, working in tandem with them, the following strategies and techniques might help the child.

At home and school:

- Maintain good lifestyle interventions – in particular healthy diet choices and exercise programmes.
- Help to support executive function skills, often considered to be a major impairment in children with ADHD (see Chapter 3),
- Establish predictability, structure and routine (see Chapter 4).
- Be consistent and firm to reinforce the routines.
- Maintain patience and a sense of humour.
- Provide a fiddle toy/focus tool – at home and school.
- Give positive and rapid feedback on activities and behaviour.

At school:

- Favourable seating in class – away from distractions and near to the teacher, so they can help to discretely refocus.
- Explain a change in routine before it happens.
- Have plenty for the pupil to do as they may well 'finish first' and be left with time to drift into disruption if not occupied fully.
- Use IT and computer-based learning as an alternative to traditional pen and paper.
- Set up an established routine for personal organisation such as recording homework and showing that it has been done.
- Break a task down into a series of smaller tasks to coincide with short attention spans.
- Make eye contact frequently with the child.
- Build in 'thinking time' if a question is asked so that there is no impulsive shouting out by such a child.
- Always maintain positive academic expectations.

Overlapping traits and characteristics in respect of the most common co-occurring conditions
ADHD and a brief overview of the most common overlapping conditions

There are thought to be genetic links between ADHD and several psychiatric conditions, including anxiety, obesity and depression (and to a lesser extent bipolar disorder and substance misuse), as well as specific learning differences and other medical conditions. One study suggested that as many as 33 per cent of children with ADHD have co-occurring difficulties with at least one learning difference, or emotional or behavioural condition (2007 National Survey of Children's Health).

When a clinician is considering diagnosis, they should also consider whether there might be any co-occurring conditions, which might be flagged by unexplained symptoms that do not automatically fall under the ADHD umbrella. If they are concerned about this, their report should signpost other professionals to consult, as well as addressing it in their recommended treatment plan.

A note about co-occurring differences in boys and girls with ADHD

Co-existing conditions should be considered the norm rather than the exception; often a contributory factor to a missed or late diagnosis of ADHD in girls is that the symptoms of the co-existing difficulty are more obvious than the ADHD symptoms, because of their general desire to conform and please, and therefore to internalise symptoms as much as possible.

The converse is true for boys – often because the symptoms of ADHD are not so readily internalised by boys, parents and teaching professionals may miss signs of co-existing difficulties.

Co-occurring conditions

There are a myriad of overlapping conditions, including:

- ◆ ASC (autism spectrum condition)
- ◆ SpLD (specific learning difference)
- ◆ Tourette's syndrome/tics
- ◆ ODD (oppositional defiance disorder)
- ◆ Anxiety
- ◆ CD (conduct disorder)
- ◆ Mood disorders/bipolar disorder
- ◆ SPD (sensory processing disorder).

The most commonly occurring of these will be explored in more detail in the following sections.

Autism spectrum condition

The overlap between ADHD and ASC (also referred to as ASD – autism spectrum disorder) is now thought to be relatively high. Before the DSM-5 (APA, 2013), ADHD and ASC were considered to be mutually exclusive, and it has only been since 2013 that co-occurrence of these conditions has become accepted, with a dual diagnosis now being possible. Now, it is estimated that 30–80 per cent of children with ASC also have ADHD, and that 20–50 per cent of children with ADHD also have ASC.

Children with ASC usually experience a triad of impairments focused on social interaction, social imagination and sensory issues and routines. They can be socially awkward and can struggle to understand and manage their own emotions.

It can be confusing to detect what characteristics your child is displaying. Both ASC and ADHD can cause social challenges. For children with ASC this is more likely to be linked to difficulties in interpreting the subtleties of verbal and non-verbal communication (language interpretation and non-spoken social cues). For children with ADHD, social challenges will arise because of impulsivity (blurting things out), inattention (not following a conversation and appearing detached) or difficulty with organising thoughts. A child with ASC who is experiencing sensory overload may present outwardly as being inattentive. Similarly, a child with ADHD may present as being socially awkward because of their impulsivity.

Common/confusing overlaps between ASC and ADHD	
Difficulties turn taking	ADHD child: because of their impulsivity
	ASC child: because they do not fully understand social norms
Responding when being called	ADHD child: because of inattention
	ASC child: because they could be in their 'own world', or have social interaction difficulties
Difficulties making and keeping friendships	ADHD child: because their impulsivity and hyperactivity can make sustaining friendships difficult
	ASC child: because of the difficulties with social interaction
Some shared executive function difficulties	See Chapter 3
Keen interest in certain topics/things	ADHD child: they can hyper-focus on things of interest
	ASC child: can have intense special interests

Oppositional defiance disorder

ODD describes a pattern of behaviours which needs to have been present for over six months and involves the child being defiant, negative or hostile.

Having a child with ODD can be very difficult for parent because in essence the child tries to 'kick-back' against authority, and appears inflexible, defiant and deliberately annoying; the child can become easily annoyed and defensive themselves, and can appear to act in a spiteful or vindictive way.

Common/confusing overlaps between ODD and ADHD	
Failure to follow instructions	ADHD child: can be too impulsive or too distracted to follow instructions; can unintentionally appear defiant ODD child: wants to be defiant
Task avoidance	ADHD child: may find it difficult to start/complete tasks because they are not able to sustain their concentration ODD child: will deliberately avoid tasks
Outbursts and interruptions	ADHD child: often does not inhibit their impulses and will unintentionally blurt out ODD child: may have chronic argumentativeness and refuse to comply with adult requests, and so might choose to interrupt as a demonstration of defiance or refusal to comply with rules
Goal-directed motivation	ADHD child: may be driven to do something that they want to do, without a wider awareness of the circumstances ODD child: may have a similar drive to do something, but with an underlying defiance

Specific learning differences

An SpLD is a difference or difficulty with a particular aspect of learning. Common SpLDs include:

- Dyslexia – a specific difficulty primarily affecting the skills of reading and writing and spelling.
- Dyspraxia/DCD (developmental coordination disorder) – difficulties primarily affecting physical coordination.
- Dyscalculia – difficulty with mathematics, primarily arithmetic, and an understanding of number.
- Dysgraphia – difficulty with written expression, primarily with writing.

Common/confusing overlaps between common SpLDs and ADHD	
Trouble organising thoughts	ADHD child: may be impulsive or distracted SpLD child: may have slow processing speed/memory recall and have trouble organising thoughts quickly enough
Finding the right word to use when speaking	ADHD child: blurts out and talks before thinking through SpLD child: may have slow processing speed/memory recall and have trouble retrieving the correct word quickly enough

Forgetfulness/ remembering lessons	ADHD child: may be forgetful, lose things and forget to be in the right place at the right time
	SpLD child: may have a vulnerability with their memory leading to difficulties recalling names, lessons and mixing up words
Difficulty with reading	ADHD child: might read slowly or skip a line of text or lose their place if they become distracted, or fail to take notice of punctuation, however they will probably read accurately
	SpLD child with dyslexia: will read slowly, but they will probably have difficulty at the word level and find it hard to read accurately
Difficulty with writing	ADHD child: may find it hard to organise their thoughts in a logical order to convey themselves well on the page; they will also find it hard to have the self-motivation to proofread for errors and meaning. Their writing might also be messy
	SpLD child with dyslexia, dysgraphia or DCD/dyspraxia may have difficulty writing or conveying themselves on the page for a number of reasons such as: the mechanics of writing is difficult for them, their spelling and grammar present a challenge, they have trouble organising thoughts, they find it hard to write neatly or proofreading is challenging because it is hard to spot their mistakes
Attention issues	ADHD child: commonly has attention difficulties as part of the condition
	SpLD child: may appear to have attention issues because of a vulnerability in working memory or speed of processing which can make them lose their place in a conversation or find it hard to keep up in a lesson, and making it appear as if they have attentional difficulties. A child with an SpLD may also get tired out because of the demand that trying to manage their SpLD places on them – they may therefore appear to zone out or lose their focus if they become overtired by the demands of the day

Conduct disorder

CD is a behavioural condition where a child displays challenging anti-social, bullying and aggressive behaviour. A diagnosis of CD requires a persistent pattern of aggression and violation of rules and people's rights to be present for at least the preceding six months; it can often begin before the age of 13. The difference between students with CD and ADHD is intent – the actions of a child with CD are likely to be pre-meditated, whereas the child with ADHD is often impulsive and thinks about the consequences after having carried out the act.

Common/confusing overlaps between CD and ADHD	
Poor inhibitory control/ decision making	ADHD child: will make poor decisions because they can be impulsive and act before thinking
	CD child: will make poor decisions wilfully or defiantly, and then might try to mount a defence and become deceitful about their actions
Sustained attention	ADHD child: has difficulty with sustaining their attention on a task, particularly if that task does not grab their attention
	CD child: can also have difficulty sustaining their attention but the underlying reason for this is different and may be anchored in wilful defiance
Cognitive switching – i.e. the process of intentionally switching attention from one task to another	ADHD child: can find it hard to mentally switch from one task to another, particularly if they are engaged with the task in hand
	CD child: can also find it hard to switch from an intentionally aggravating activity to another less emotive one

Tics and Tourette's syndrome

Tics are a condition of the nervous system where a child exhibits involuntary sounds, rapid movements, or twitches. Research suggests that tics are an inherited genetic condition. Tourette's syndrome is a severe version of a tic – usually consisting of motor and vocal tics which have been present for over one year.

Fewer than 10 per cent of individuals with ADHD have Tourette's; however, 60–80 per cent of children with Tourette's syndrome also have ADHD.

Tics usually occur several/many times a day and can be simple, small movements like sniffing, grunting, coughing or blinking; they can also consist of repeated words or phrases, or larger body movements.

Common/confusing overlaps between tics/Tourette's and ADHD	
Sounds or movements	ADHD child: can often repeat a physical movement – such as continually jigging their leg when seated. These movements help to stimulate the production of dopamine, accepted as under-stimulated in an ADHD child. An ADHD child can also blurt out random sounds because they have poor impulse control
	Tics or Tourette's syndrome: child makes movements or noises involuntarily, but for different reasons to that of ADHD, and they are involuntary

Mood disorders and bipolar disorder

It is not uncommon for someone with ADHD to have a mood disorder at some point in their life – it is said people with ADHD are three times more likely to experience a mood disorder than a neurotypical person. Common shared features can include feelings of anxiety, low mood, lack of focus and poor sleep.

Some experts hypothesise that as many as 70 per cent of those with ADHD will be treated at some point in their lives for primary depression either as its own standalone illness, or for secondary depression caused by the experience of living with ADHD.

Bipolar disorder falls under the umbrella term of mood disorder, and it is characterised by mood swings – high, euphoric periods (mania) and low periods of depression – each lasting for weeks at a time. Up to 20 per cent of those with ADHD also have bipolar disorder.

Common/confusing overlaps between mood disorders/bipolar disorder and ADHD	
Inattention/poor concentration Poor appetite or over-eating Sleep problems Feelings of sadness Frequent anxiety Lack of motivation Low self-esteem/feelings of hopelessness	ADHD child: these symptoms are common features of ADHD Mood disorder and bipolar child: may lack motivation because of diminished drive to do anything at all
Bipolar – mania stage	Sometimes misinterpreted as hyperactivity
Bipolar – low states	Sometimes misinterpreted as inattention and lack of motivation

TEN TOP TIPS

In terms of diagnosis, it is important for us to keep in mind that the symptoms of ADHD, such as concentration problems and hyperactivity, can be confused with other disorders and medical problems, including learning disabilities and emotional issues, which require totally differ-ent treatments. Just because it looks like ADHD doesn't mean it is, so here are some top tips in terms of pursuing a diagnosis.

1. Make an appointment with a specialist. As the parent, you can initiate testing for ADHD on behalf of your child. The earlier you schedule this appointment, the sooner you can get help for their ADHD.

2. Speak to your child's school. Call your child's teacher or senior teacher and speak directly and openly about your pursuit of a diagnosis. Schools are required by law to assist you, and the staff will want to help improve your child's life at school.

3. Give professionals the full picture. When you are asked the tough questions about your child's behaviour, be sure to answer honestly. Your complete and truthful perspective is very important to the evaluation process.

4. Keep things moving. You are your child's advocate, and have the power to prevent delays in obtaining a diagnosis. Check in with doctors or specialists appropriately often to see where you are in the process.

5. If necessary, get a second opinion. If there is any doubt that your child has received a thorough or appropriate evaluation, you can seek another specialist's help.

6. It's normal to feel upset or intimidated by a diagnosis of ADHD. But keep in mind that getting a diagnosis can be the first step towards making life better. Once you know what you're dealing with, you can start getting treatment – and that means taking control of symptoms and feeling more confident in every area of life.

7. An ADHD diagnosis may feel like a label, but it may be more helpful to think of it as an explanation. The diagnosis explains why you may have struggled with life skills such as paying attention, following directions, listening closely, organisation – things that seem to come easily to other people.

8. Often getting a diagnosis can be a relief. You can rest easier knowing that it wasn't laziness or a lack of intelligence standing in your or your child's way, but rather a difference or a disorder that you can learn how to manage.

9. Keep in mind that an ADHD diagnosis is not a sentence for a lifetime of suffering. Some people have only mild symptoms, while others experience more pervasive problems. But regardless of

where your child is on this spectrum, there are many steps you can take to manage the symptoms.

10. Co-existing conditions with ADHD often occur. In many cases ADHD may overlap with other conditions such as depression, dyslexia, oppositional defiant disorder and autistic spectrum disorder. Try not to feel intimidated or overwhelmed and look at the situation as the first step in the journey to be able to better understand and support your child.

See Appendix 3 for a link to an online child ADHD screener tool - it will be one of many, so do take a look at what else is on offer online.

AND ALSO...

The key to remember is that ADHD is treatable. Don't give up hope. With the right treatment and support, your child will be able to get the symptoms of ADHD under control and build the life that they want. It's up to you to take action to manage the symptoms of ADHD. Health professionals can help, but ultimately the responsibility lies in your own hands.

Chapter 3

EXECUTIVE FUNCTION SKILLS

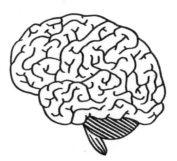

In this chapter we will consider:

- ♦ what executive function skills (EFs) are
- ♦ how to identify and explain the individual EFs
- ♦ strategies for each EF.

Reference has been made in the previous chapters to executive function skills (EFs); it is commonly accepted that executive function difficulties are tightly linked with ADHD (but not exclusively so, as we all have strengths and weaknesses in our EFs). In this chapter we are going to explore what EFs are and how they impact individuals with ADHD.

What are EFs?

In essence EFs are the self-management system of the brain, and children with ADHD usually have weaker executive functions when compared to their peers and their age and stage of development. Executive functions underly all social and academic behaviours. They are a group of brain-based processes which control our:

1. thoughts
2. actions
3. feelings.

This helps us to:

1. hold information in mind
2. think flexibly
3. control our impulses.

These are all key skills which are often impacted in children with ADHD. EFs are controlled by the pre-frontal cortex of the brain, which regulates attention, behaviour and impulsivity, and which features prominently in the neurological underpinning for ADHD. It is sometimes described as the 'thinking' part of the brain, and is the last part of the brain to develop (thought to be well into our twenties).

It is important to remember when looking at EFs that not all parts of the pre-frontal cortex – or to put it in another way, not all parts of the neural networks of the brain – are impacted for each individual in the same way. This explains why ADHD can present so differently from person to person, and why EFs strengths and challenges can vary so much from person to person too.

Emotional regulation

Emotional regulation is perhaps one of the key factors that affects children with ADHD. Neurotypical individuals tend to be able to regulate their emotions; and if you are in control of your emotions as opposed to being controlled by them, you are far more likely and able to pursue your goals. This is because your ability to self-regulate your emotional state enables you to push aside certain emotions so that you can sustain your attention to do the things that you need or want to do to achieve goals and positive outcomes. If you flip this explanation on its head, it is easy to see why emotionally dysregulated children who have ADHD will struggle.

In order to maintain our emotional equilibrium, different parts of the brain are involved:

- The **limbic system**, which is controlled by the **amygdala**, is in charge of our emotional and behavioural responses. The is the first part of the brain to develop in babyhood, and it controls our primitive emotional response system – it is not moderated, meaning it just responds – and it controls our flight, fight or freeze response to danger. This was important when we lived in caves and needed to be able to respond to imminent danger very quickly, because the 'flight, fight or freeze' part of our brain instantly takes control in these situations. Although we have evolved and moved out of caves, this part of the brain has not, and it continues to respond to perceived dangers present in our modern world. In order to live a well-balanced and regulated life, as long as we are safe, we do not want to engage the limbic system of our brain.
- The **pre-frontal cortex** provides this balance – it is the 'reasoning' part of the brain, and it develops last – into our mid-twenties. The EFs develop in the pre-frontal cortex, and it is this skillset that helps us to moderate and control our emotions, and enables us to make good judgement calls.
- In a neurotypical brain, when these two areas of the brain work together, the ability to moderate emotions continues to improve, because, as we have just discovered, EFs continue to mature into adulthood.

However, for the ADHD brain, recent developments and advances in fMRI imaging have shown us that the pre-frontal cortex does not develop at the same rate as someone without ADHD. Therefore, it is thought that ADHD children and teenagers often operate in terms of their executive functioning some two to three years (sometimes even four years) behind their neurotypical peers. Thus, when children with ADHD are accused of being emotionally dysregulated, it is because of this delay in the development and maturation of the ADHD brain, and they are not doing it 'on purpose'.

In summary, it is often the case that ADHD children do not possess the EF skills that they need for their growing independence – yet!!

- It is important to understand that socially and emotionally your child's EFs maturity may be two to four years behind their peers. Therefore, we should not expect age-appropriate rational decision making in a 14-year-old who might be operating as a 12-year-old, or even a 20-year-old who might still be operating as a 16-year-old. Their EFs, which are controlled by their pre-frontal cortex, are not fully developed yet – we just have to wait it out.
- The good news for children with ADHD is that EF weaknesses can be supported and improved throughout childhood and adolescence. This is because EFs are controlled by a part of the brain called the frontal lobe, or the pre-frontal cortex, which is the last part of the brain to fully develop and reach maturity – and it is thought that this reaching of maturity does not occur until an individual is in their twenties.
- The pre-frontal cortex is not fully developed or mature until the nerves in this part of the brain are fully myelinated, or insulated, and it is this myelination or 'insulation' of the synapses that increases the rate at which electrical impulses are sent and received, and can flow freely.
- When trying to strengthen EFs, we need to remember that the more we repeat an activity or 'good practice' the more we reinforce the desired outcome, and therefore the more we are helping the process of myelination, or insulation of those particular synapses that help responses to become automatic. It is said that we need to do approximately 60 iterations of something before it becomes a habit!

All this adds up to mean that strategies can be put in place to strengthen EFs throughout the educational life of a young person.

Identify and explain the individual EFs

As already identified, EFs are a set of mental or cognitive skills required to self-regulate, manage behaviours, get things done and balance our needs and desires. Different experts have differing views on how many EFs there are. Our view on the number and types of EFs is detailed here:

Overview of executive function skills		
EF	**Explanation**	**Examples of EF weakness**
Response or impulse inhibition	Thinking before you act	• Acting before you think • Not thinking about the consequences
Working memory	Holding information in the memory while performing a task (including drawing on past experiences to inform the present or future)	• Losing track of your possessions and where you have put them • Difficulty remembering what you have to do • Not learning from experience
Flexibility	Being able to adapt your plans in the face of changing circumstances – when new information comes to light, new obstacles crop up or setbacks occur	• Becoming upset if things do not go according to plan • 'Going with the flow' is the ability to adapt to changing situations, a difficulty with flexibility may result in tantrums or anxiety when things change unexpectedly
Sustained attention	The ability to keep paying attention despite feeling tired, bored or distracted	• Starting something and not finishing it • Being hassled by parents to persevere and complete homework
Task initiation	The ability to get on and start projects without procrastinating	• Difficulty stopping something you are interested in to prioritise a less appealing task or work • Putting off getting started
Planning/ prioritisation	Being able to plan and prioritise what to do to achieve a goal, and focusing on what is important to achieve it	• Not being able to see what you need to do to achieve a goal • Not knowing where or how to start a task
Organisation	Having systems and routines to keep track of information and belongings	• Always losing things or not being able to find things • Chaotic note-keeping systems • Messy bag or backpack
Time management	Having a concept of time and a sense that time is important. Being able to estimate how much time something will take, and the ability to meet deadlines	• Being late for lessons • Under-estimating how long homework will take • Not being aware of the passage of time when doing something pleasurable – like gaming • Difficulty maintaining routines and deadlines

Goal-directed persistence	Having a goal and being able to pursue it through to its completion	• Giving up when the going gets tough
Metacognition	Being able to stand back and look at yourself and self-evaluate how you operate/problem-solve	• Not understanding how you learn • Not being able to engage in 'self-talk' and asking yourself 'how am I doing?'

Difficulties with some (or all) of these skillsets may well sound familiar, but it's important to remember that the pre-frontal cortex, which controls these skills, is still developing in children and adolescents and therefore any deficits can be supported and improved!

The first step, as parents, that we need to take is to try to coach our children to develop some of these skills, because it is *they* who need to be able to do this, and not us! This means that we must try to stop organising and problem-solving for our child – in other words, we need to stop trying to be the child's pre-frontal cortex, and we need to encourage them to develop their own EF skills. However, the way in which we do this must be gradual and scaffolded. We cannot suddenly withdraw our support and expect them to get on with it, much as we would not remove stabilisers too early and expect our child to be able to ride a bike unaided. The frontal lobes of the brain (pre-frontal cortex) need to be trained to become the 'executives in charge': you need to continue to offer support to your child as you try to transfer your good leadership and organisation skills to them, so that their pre-frontal cortex is not left unstructured and inefficient!

How might EF weaknesses manifest themselves – or how can you begin to recognise EF challenges in your child?

- Your son/daughter may give in to having meltdowns (response inhibition/emotional control) about homework because they are at home, and they are not trying to 'hold it together' in front of their class.
- During the normal school day, pupils receive a lot of discreet assistance from members of the school community (with task initiation, planning/prioritisation, organisation, time management), to help them 'keep on track'. When this scaffolding is not there, in the evenings/holidays etc., they may find it more difficult to organise themselves and get on with and complete work.

- Your child might have a low awareness of themselves and their ability to self-monitor and to problem-solve (metacognition).
- Transitions, navigating the school day, moving between lessons and unexpected changes in routine might be challenging for your child (flexibility).
- Without the stimulation of being in school, with a teacher teaching, and classmates interacting, your child may find it more difficult to maintain their level of engagement (sustained attention) to complete homework in a timely manner (prioritisation and task initiation).
- Your child may struggle to retain information or instructions in their minds whilst performing tasks (working memory).
- Or your child may find it hard to complete a task that they are not particularly interested in (goal-directed persistence).

It is perfectly normal to be better at some of these skills than others. It becomes challenging when some/all of these skills are sufficiently tricky for an individual that they begin to dominate life.

Because everybody, and in particular individuals with ADHD, have strengths and weaknesses within their EF profile we will now take a look in a bit more depth at each of the individual EFs, to help you assess where your son or daughter's strengths and weaknesses lie, and how you might help scaffold them to develop some of their more vulnerable EF skills.

Strategies to support the individual EFs
Response inhibition

Response inhibition is the ability to think before you act, or to stop, change or inhibit a response that has already begun. Poor response inhibition includes behaviours such as blurting things out and reacting in the heat of the moment.

A difficulty with inhibiting responses resonates for people with ADHD because it is linked to impatience and impulsivity, and this makes it difficult to pause and engage in self-talk, e.g. 'that behaviour/response/reaction is too much, let me tone that down'.

For individuals with ADHD, it is extremely hard to inhibit responses to stimuli when experiencing emotional dysregulation. Emotional dys-regulation can escalate quickly, and it can take time for an individual to come back down to a baseline. This can be exacerbated by some trigger events such as:

- **Transitioning to secondary school.** In secondary school there are increased social and academic demands, and more projects that require long-term planning. A move to secondary school also often brings with it a desire for greater independence. Therefore, decreasing parental scaffolding (which up until this point has created routine and made life more predictable for your child, but suddenly becomes less acceptable to them) creates more opportunities for things to 'go wrong' and for emotional dysregulation to kick in. Ironically, however, despite this desire for independence, ADHD teens need more support than neurotypical children.
- **The teenage years.** At this point in their lives children also start having to deal with puberty and raging hormones, meaning that they are prone to having heightened emotions. It is important to remember that girls can have a monthly exacerbation of ADHD symptoms when their oestrogen levels are low.

These additional factors, or triggers, in an individual's life will mean that response inhibition can become even more challenging to control!

Home can often be the environment where this dysregulation is 'acted out'. This is because at home children do not have to 'hold it together' in the same way as they do in front of their peers at school, therefore they may manage their behaviour and reactions less well when they are in their 'safe' environment. Thus, family members can often feel the brunt of dysregulation more keenly than those outside of the home – the teen can have unfettered meltdowns, and may act more foolishly than they might otherwise. In other words, they may not inhibit their responses very well whilst at home.

It is thought by some ADHD specialists that response inhibition is one of the most important EFs to try to scaffold, because if an individual has under-developed self-help strategies, meaning their reaction to external triggers is not controlled properly, they will regularly experience emotional dysregulation; and the knock-on effect is that heightened emotional dysregulation makes it even harder to stay in control of the other EFs.

As parents, it is important for us to know how to help our child to develop strategies to recognise this dysregulation within themselves, and to help them to overcome it. One way of doing this is to brainstorm the likely triggers and develop a routine for your child to work to address the issue – whilst this can be chatted through, a visual will probably have a more lasting impact and will be something your child can refer back to time and again, whereas they may struggle to recall a conversation.

Therefore, together with your child, you could create a Response Inhibition Problem-Solving worksheet:

Response Inhibition Problem-Solving worksheet

1. Discuss, identify and make a note of any areas where your child struggles to control their responses.
   - For example: getting angry quickly, getting anxious in certain situations, blurting things out, interrupting conversations, over-exuberant reactions, overwhelmed by anger, sadness, even hilarity – or whatever other 'response inhibition' your child experiences.

2. Encourage your child to learn how to 'self-talk' – so that when a situation arises, they learn to pause and say to themselves 'Good choice/bad choice?' They will need to practise how to stop and think, and you will need to encourage them to reflect afterwards, so that they can begin to learn from their mistakes. It will be important to discuss plausible solutions with your child. By doing this you are helping your child to think about the things that might be causing them some difficulty, but without it being in the heat of the moment – therefore their more 'rational' brain should be able to come up with some good solutions. By recording these solutions in a chart (rather than relying on a conversation), your child can refer to the visual representation, when the rational side of their brain has been overtaken by impulsivity.
   - For example: 'I can help control my response of getting anxious about...by asking my teacher to...'

3. Ask your child to choose the solutions that they prefer. It is best for them to do this, as it will be more meaningful for them.
   - For example: 'Best option – I won't blurt out my answer by counting to five before I speak.'

4. Talk about what will happen if the first solution does not work.
   - For example: 'My best option didn't work, so I instead of calling out I will write my answers on a sticky note and show it to my teacher who has told me for every three written answers I hand in I will get a house point.'

5. Make a visual reminder/chart with your child recording the steps they need to go through to self-regulate, so that your child can refer to it to remind themselves about their strategies in the future.
   - See below for an example of a worksheet:

What is the problem?
e.g. I get panicky if I don't know how to do a homework that's been set

---

What are some possible things I could do to solve the problem?

1. Take deep breaths to try to calm myself down.
2. Think about what buddies I can use to help me. Consider how I will ask them to help me?
3. Send the teacher an email to tell them I've got a bit lost in the lesson and ask for clarification about homework.
4. ... (whatever strategies work for the teenager).

What will I try first?

List the priorities 1, 2, 3.

If this doesn't work what can I do? E.g.:

1. I know I can use my group-chat and ask my classmates (who might not be in my friends group) to explain what the homework was.
2. Go to see the teacher before the next lesson and ask them for some time to explain the task

How did it go? Did my solution work?

What might I do differently next time?

It will be important to acknowledge with your child that they will still be impulsive and have poor impulse control at times, and that is OK. But each successful response inhibition should be acknowledged and praised, to reinforce their achievement. Eventually they should learn to give themselves a metaphorical pat on the back when they do exert some impulse control – but remember, this will probably need to be modelled by you, until they get into the habit themselves of practising positive 'self-talk'.

Flexibility

Flexibility is the ability to adapt and revise plans when conditions change; e.g. when obstacles and setbacks arise, or when new information becomes available, or when mistakes occur. It is the ability to 'go with the flow' and not get thrown by last-minute changes.

Exercising flexibility means that instead of being disappointed or upset when changes arise, you are able to start thinking about how you can solve the problem and find ways around it.

Areas of education in which you might notice your child having issues with flexibility include:

- Struggling with assignments that require creativity or are open-ended.
- Getting stuck on one solution or one way of looking at a problem.

- Having trouble coming up with topics or ideas for things to write about.
- Having difficulty coming up with 'plan B' if the first attempt did not work.
- Finding it hard to deal with changes in plans or routines.
- Finding it difficult to cope with open-ended prep assignments (e.g. they don't know what to write about, or where to start).

Ideas about how to help with flexibility difficulties

- Whenever possible, provide advance notice or warning of what's coming next – perhaps make time to look at your child's timetable together at the beginning of the day, and plot out the transitions and expected events – but each time reinforce to them that there may be last-minute adaptations; that way the concept of change becomes part of your regular conversation.
- Try to maintain schedules and routines whenever possible, whilst building in the possibility of flexibility – e.g. try to discuss with your child the requirement to check their school email/school notification system during the day, in case a change is noted. Sow the seed with your child that they need to be prepared for something like this, if it happens.
- In general, help your child to anticipate what they might encounter in a situation – the more information they have in advance the more they will feel able to cope and navigate the unexpected situation.
- If you know what causes your child anxiety (a missed lesson or work notification, not understanding a homework task) walk and talk them through the anxiety-producing situation, so you can discuss it and confront it together, and come up with some strategies to manage it.
- Help your child come up with a few default strategies for handling situations where flexibility causes the most problems – this can include simple things like walking away from the situation for some cool-off time, and then returning and asking a specific person for help.

So that your child is able to develop some independence to deal with flexibility on their own, without you needing to scaffold them, encourage them to:

- Notice any physical warning signs of inflexibility (muscle tightness, breathing changes) and encourage them to ask themselves if this particular situation is a big deal or little deal to them – and depending on their reaction, whether they can find a way to be flexible.
- Encourage them to think about what could go wrong, and what their 'plan B' might be.
- Encourage them to think about whether there is another way to think about a scenario that they are finding difficult to handle.

Task initiation

Task initiation is the ability to begin projects or activities without procrastination, in an efficient and timely manner. Using this skill can involve beginning a task as soon as it is assigned or deciding when a task will be done and beginning promptly at a predetermined time.

Difficulties with task initiation include:

- Procrastinating/avoiding tasks due to:
  - not knowing how to get started
  - believing the task will 'take forever'
  - believing your performance won't meet expectations
  - seeing the task as tedious, boring, irrelevant.
- Finding other things to do rather than start schoolwork.
- Difficulty getting back to work after breaks.

Children can often over-estimate how much time they have to do a task in and under-estimate how long the task will actually take. They will often also choose to complete an interesting or fun activity both as a way to gain some immediate pleasure and as a way of avoiding or escaping the non-preferred task.

Ideas about how to help with task initiation difficulties

- Whenever possible use a work goal that your child has been encouraged to set themselves (rather than one imposed on them). However, if the goal/end result is far off in the future, or the number of tasks involved in achieving the goal is large, beginning the task may still be a problem.

- If a task seems overwhelming, encourage your son/daughter to work with you or their teacher to break the task down into more manageable parts, with specific deadlines for each part.
- Where possible try to let your child decide on deadlines and cuing systems that work best for them in order to trigger a willingness to engage in task initiation.
- When the ball is rolling, keep it going – stopping and starting can be the enemy of task initiation, so if your child has successfully started on a task and they have the momentum and perseverance to be able to keep going, encourage them to do so, reminding them that it will get the job done more quickly and drag the task out less.
- Trying to stay positive will help your child engage more with task initiation.

Help your child to identify task initiation difficulties (for non-preferred tasks) to help increase their self-awareness of what possible triggers are by discussing with them and encouraging them to self-reflect about:

- whether they put off homework or chores until the last minute
- whether it is hard for them to put aside fun activities to start schoolwork
- whether they need lots of reminders to start activities.

To help your child improve their task avoidance, you will need to model and promote their self-talk, so that they can overcome obstacles and knuckle down and get going. You will need to encourage them to engage in an internal conversation along the lines of:

- This is the first step; all I need to do is start.
- I will just start with... (a small chunk of the whole task).
- I will work for (a defined amount of time).
- If I don't take this step, I won't get any closer to finishing/achieving my goal.

Often if you can break down the barrier to just getting started, a bit of momentum builds and the child can work a bit longer than they thought – and if they cannot, they go through the process again for the next chunk of the task.

Sustained attention

Sustained attention is the capacity to keep focusing on a situation or task in hand in spite of distractions, fatigue or boredom. This means being able to maintain attention in class, persevere with prep and complete any chores you set. If sustained attention is weak, you will be conscious that your child may need directions/instructions to be repeated and that they are frequently 'off task'. You may also be aware of your child jumping from one task to another and often failing to complete the preceding task before choosing to move on to a second. Your child may also look for distractions such as checking their phone every few minutes.

It should be noted that as a generation, it is possible that our children have less capacity for sustained attention than previous generations, in part because of the fast-paced technological world in which they live, where things seem designed for instant gratification rather than sustained attention and perseverance.

Working at home – doing homework or revision – can highlight difficulties with sustained attention, because your child will be working on their own and will not have the external stimuli of classmates to help keep them motivated, or against whom to compare their own ability to concentrate.

What you might see in your child if they have difficulty with sustained attention:

- taking frequent breaks when working
- taking breaks that are too long
- being internally distracted – by thoughts, states, moods, daydreams
- being externally distracted – by sights, sounds, technology (phone, computer, TV, video games etc.)
- not knowing limits (e.g. how long they can sustain attention) or when the best time to study is
- not recognising for themselves when they are off task.

Ideas about how to help with sustained attention difficulties

- Try to encourage your child to identify particular tasks (e.g. homework) that are tough to focus on, and talk to them about whether there are ways to modify the tasks (such as breaking them into smaller parts) that would help them to maintain attention and complete the task.

- Provide supervision, by checking in with your child periodically to see how they are doing, or to help them put the distractions to one side.
- Try to have a discussion about how long your child feels they can work on a task before needing a break and then discuss whether a timer would be a good idea to depict elapsed time (children often can have a distorted sense of the passage of time, particularly if it is a task they are reluctant to do).
- A regular, very brief alarm/agreed upon cue can be effective to help your child refocus, if sustained attention is a particular problem area for them.
- Use incentive systems – e.g. 'first – then' plans, whereby they complete the less preferred activity first and can then move on to a more preferred one.
- Always give praise for staying on task and for successfully completing a task (instead of negative connotations – e.g. child perceiving that you nag them to get work done).

Some of the things that you will need to discuss with them and encourage them to think about are:

- Is it more difficult to sustain attention with some subjects than others?
- What kind of internal conversation does your child have with themselves that leads them to either give up or to stick with it?
- Does the length of the piece of work make a difference to your child's ability to complete it?

It will also be important for you to help your child to identify:

- What kinds of things distract them?
- Is there a place to study which they find minimises their distractions?
- How do they manage the distractions when they occur?

Once you have been able to have this kind of conversation with them, you can then go on to help them by:

- setting realistic work goals and encouraging them to stick to them
- establishing when to take planned breaks and then getting back to work on schedule
- encouraging them to get into the routine of gathering all necessary materials before beginning a task, so that there are no obstacles and distractions to hinder progress once they have started.

You will need to help promote the concept of working first and then playing/resting etc. afterwards. If you are able to help your child to build in their own personal rewards for completing tasks (such as a short stint on social media for completing something for example), this will build their independence at taking control of their attention and focus. They will need help until they learn the routine that once the reward is over, they then need to get back to work.

Planning and prioritisation

Planning/prioritisation is the ability to create a set of steps to reach a goal or complete a task, coupled with the ability to focus on what is most important along the way.

When you have formulated a good plan, you know how to focus on what's most important and you know to let the little things go.

What you might see in your child if they have difficulties with planning and prioritisation:

- not making a study plan (not knowing how)
- not being able to break long-term projects into smaller tasks and timelines
- having difficulty taking notes or studying for tests – finding it difficult to decipher the important from the unimportant
- spending too much time on less important elements – finding it difficult to put the most important jobs first
- planning unrealistically (e.g. failing to take into account obstacles to the plan).

Ideas about how to help with planning and prioritisation difficulties

- Encourage your child to plan – and include them as much as possible in the planning process for tasks that you might plan together.
- If your child appears to understand the various pieces of a project that needs to get done, but isn't sure how to get started, prompt them to prioritise by asking what needs to get done as the first step, next step and so on in the process.
- The best approach to help your child develop organisational skills is to approach it from an area that they have an investment in.
- In the short term offer your child reminders (that they can tolerate) about their organisation, even though your goal is to be able to withdraw those reminders in due course.
- Offering to help your child clean and organise their space from time to time can be helpful.
- Where possible try to model some simple organisational operations for your child. Try to share examples from your own life.

Ways you can help your child to develop self-help strategies include:

- helping them to create 'planning forms' to help keep them on track
- encouraging them to ask teachers to tell them/help to identify the most important points and concepts to focus on when studying for a test/producing a project
- talking about what comes first, next and after that, and what they need to give up to get there
- when they are given instructions for tasks and projects, encourage them to underline and number each instruction so that it becomes an action to be completed.

Here are some ideas about planning and prioritisation worksheets your child can adapt to make their own:

Identifying tasks and due dates

What do I need to do? (List each step in order)	When will I do it?	Check off when done
1.		
2.		
3.		
4.		

Reminder list

Include here any additional tasks or details you need to keep in mind as you work. Cross out or check each one off as you do it

1.

2.

3.

4.

5.

6.

7.

Daily reminders – things I cannot forget

Monday	Tuesday	Wednesday	Thursday	Friday	Saturday	Sunday

Organisation

Organisation is the ability to create and maintain a system for arranging and keeping track of important things.

Keeping track of things and having a reasonably organised bedroom and work environment increases efficiency by eliminating the need to waste lots of time looking for things; they can just get ready to work on a task or project. This in turn reduces stress.

If your child has a tendency to over-estimate how much time they have, and to under-estimate how much time a task will take, they may be operating quite close to the edge to begin with, and not being able to find essential materials is an unnecessary and avoidable stress that might send them spiralling into orbit.

As parents we try to step back from close monitoring of our children, and we hope to be able to progress to occasionally providing a prompt or nudge. Some children, however, will need more guidance and scaffolding than others, before that support structure is gently removed.

What you might see in a child who has poor organisational skills is:

- not using or knowing how to design an organisational system
- not being able to find things in notebooks or backpacks
- not having a neat study area
- losing electronic data – forgetting where work is stored or what name it's filed under.

Good organisational skills will look like:

- a tidy desk, locker, bedroom so your child can find things when they need them
- making numbers and calculations orderly and easy to follow in maths
- being able to write so that ideas on one topic are all in one section or paragraph.

Difficulties with organisation might include:

- misplaced work
- a cluttered desk
- messy workspace

- misplaced information
- disorganised school bag
- belongings left around the house
- losing things.

How to help your child stay organised and keep track of materials

1. Have a system to help them to store their schoolwork – in folders or books depending on the teachers' preferences.
2. Encourage them to write any INCOMPLETE WORK in an organiser and keep a note in it of any tasks that are set, as soon as they are set – also note the due date.
3. Encourage your child to write the DUE DATE for tasks on the top of the task sheet itself, as soon as they get it.
4. As soon as they finish an assignment, mark it off as completed, and file the completed work away.
5. Encourage them to keep all work teachers want them to keep, filed away properly. Throw out pieces of paper that they do not have to keep – get them to check with the teacher if they are unsure.
6. Encourage them to have/develop a system for keeping their work materials (such as pens, pencils, erasers and calculators etc.) tidy.
7. If they are creative, they can make themselves useful 'organisers' from household recycling – cleaned out tins for different items of stationery like colouring pens, pencils, rulers etc.; creating organisers/planners, using colour coding to help organise books by subject; covered cereal boxes with a large side removed as a 'to do' box/filing system.
8. Encourage your child to remove unnecessary items or clutter from their room/workspace.
9. Get your child to get ready for things the night before (laying out clothes, getting ready for the next day's remote learning).
10. Use memory aids (visual aids/checklists).
11. Label and colour code things.
12. Encourage them to observe what organised people do...

Encourage your child to use their phone/tablet to set reminders or to use the latest apps to help with organisation.

Time management

Time management is actually composed of other executive skills – task initiation, sustained attention and planning – as well as 'time estimation'. Many pupils have trouble with time management because they have trouble with estimating how long something will take. The most frequent difficulty is under-estimating how long something will take and therefore not allowing enough time to complete it. Sometimes, conversely, pupils will over-estimate how long something will take and this can then make the task seem overwhelming, and so it becomes difficult to start.

Time estimation can be improved through practice, so a good habit to get into is estimating how long you think a task will take and then comparing it to how long it actually does take. Tracking your estimations helps to improve your concept of time.

What you might see in a child who has poor time management skills is:

- difficulty estimating how long a task will take – due to:
  - over-estimating how long it will take to do a task (therefore never getting started)
  - under-estimating how long it will take to do a task (therefore running out of time)
- being chronically late getting ready for school/obligations/appointments
- difficulty juggling multiple tasks and responsibilities because they are not managing their time properly
- a lack of a sense of urgency/not appreciating that deadlines are important
- relying on a deadline as an activator and motivator (and leaving things to the last minute in order to feel motivated by a very short deadline, to complete things).

What poor time management might look like:

- trouble sticking to a timeline
- problems estimating how long it will take to finish something (school-based tasks/prep)
- putting off studying/not studying at all
- 'wasting' time (e.g. hanging out with friends, playing computer games, social media, TV)

- putting off doing homework at night and rushing to get it done before class
- being slow to get ready for things (school, appointments, etc.).

Ideas about how to help with time management difficulties

- Try to encourage your child to stick to a routine, particularly for studying, but also for sleep and other daily routines.
- Encourage your child to make a commitment with you to follow a schedule. You may put this on the fridge or other obvious place as a reminder. You may also need (initially) to give your child reminders, when the time comes to do something.
- Encourage your child to set alarms or use apps or programs on phones etc., to help them get started on time.
- Create checklists and 'to do' lists with your child that include start times and an estimate of how long it will take. Add up how long the tasks will take and delete some for another time/day if the list is not realistic.

Pomodoro is an app that can help with breaking tasks into segments – there are others available too.

Working memory

Working memory is short-term memory (as opposed to long-term memory which is much more permanent), and it allows you store and use key pieces of information. Not only does it allow you to hold onto something in your memory for a period of time, you hold onto it long enough to be able to manipulate the information received – for example remembering and following the directions to someone's house.

Working memory is holding information in mind for brief periods of time but also manipulating it further; for example, solving a mental arithmetic calculation or following a series of verbal instructions to complete a task in a science lesson.

What you might see in a child who has poor working memory:

- writing instructions without enough detail to understand later
- forgetting to take home necessary materials, or forgetting to take materials to class

- forgetting to hand in homework
- forgetting long-term projects or upcoming tests
- difficulty following instructions
- not paying attention to classroom instructions/task directions
- trouble remembering multiple directions or multiple problem steps
- losing materials
- forgetting to complete assignments
- not recording when an assignment is due
- forgetting where things have been put
- thinking that they will remember – and then forgetting.

Ideas about how to help with working memory difficulties

- Try to make eye contact with your child before telling them something you want them to remember.
- Try to avoid external distractions when giving your child directions.
- If you are not sure whether your child has really heard/listened to you, ask them to paraphrase what you have said back to you.
- Use written reminders – lists, sticky notes, calendars etc.
- Encourage your child to use technological solutions to aid working memory by setting reminders of specific events (using apps, smartphones, digital calendars).
- When your child is going to be involved in an activity or task that they have had experience of before, reinforce their prior successes as a way of reminding them to draw on their past experiences.

Strategies to help with working memory include:

- Encourage your child to 'teach you' (e.g. get them to practise explaining a skill or activity) – this helps them to remember all the steps needed to complete the task.
- Work on visualisation skills (encourage your child to try to create a visual picture in their head of what they have just heard/want to remember).
- Play games that use visual memory (Pairs, Kim's Game, I Spy, puzzles, Spot the Difference).
- Play card games (Crazy Eights, Uno, Go Fish etc.).

- Regularly complete Sudokus, crosswords etc.
- Practise active reading strategies (taking notes, using sticky notes, asking questions as they are reading etc.).
- Use coloured markers to highlight instructions (use different colours to signal different things, such as green for the most important, red for things you might be likely to forget).
- Set reminders with time and sound cues on your smartphone.

Metacognition

Metacognition refers to the ability to stand back and observe yourself from the outside – i.e. how you problem-solve and decide what is called for in a given situation. When you have this skill, you can make decisions about how to proceed based on what you understand about yourself. Whilst doing this you ask yourself 'How am I doing?' Afterwards you evaluate how you did and then decide how to do things differently in the future.

Metacognition is a skill based on a combination of understanding your own behaviour and past experiences, as well as monitoring your behaviour as you adjust to some current new situation.

What you might see in a child who has a poor metacognitive awareness:

- They cannot accurately evaluate skills (e.g. expecting to do well in tests, despite poor past performance/preparation).
- They cannot identify appropriate study strategies.
- They cannot plan or organise a written piece of work.
- They can memorise facts but miss the larger context (they do better on multiple choice tests than essay questions).
- They have a hard time understanding more abstract concepts (maths as well as content-area subjects).
- They have difficulty making inferences, drawing conclusions, grasping the main idea, reading between the lines.
- They fail to check work/proofread to make sure they've followed the rules and haven't made careless mistakes.
- They struggle to follow directions (e.g. forgetting to do part of the assignment and losing points as a result).
- They aren't sure what to study, or how to study.
- They don't understand the material.

Ideas about how to help with metacognition difficulties

- Provide specific praise for task performance, by recognising strategies that your child uses – e.g. for chores, performance on schoolwork, interactions with friends etc. Provide specific praise such as 'you're good at understanding your friends' feelings'.
- Encourage your child to evaluate their own performance on a task or in a social situation.
- Encourage your child to ask teachers for feedback as a way to improve performance.
- Use your behaviour as a way of indirectly helping your child understand how people might react to their behaviour.

Strategies to help your child:

- Ask teachers for revision sheets for tests.
- Encourage your child to create study-packs for tests by pulling together all the important material, amalgamating and condensing notes.
- Encourage your child to create self-monitoring checklists (e.g. a proofreading checklist; see below).
- Encourage your child to ask themselves four self-monitoring questions: What is my problem? What is my plan? Am I following my plan? How did I do?

Other strategies:

- Proofreading checklist for use while checking work:
  - Do all sentences begin with a capital letter?
  - Have all proper nouns got capital letters?
  - Are all sentences complete sentences?
  - Did I use appropriate paragraphs with one key idea per paragraph?
  - Do all sentences have ending punctuation? (. ! ?)
  - Did I use commas and quotation marks correctly?
  - Did I spell every word correctly?
- Three-colour highlighting – highlight the following with a different colour for each:

- main points (often the first or last paragraph in a section or the first sentence in a paragraph)
- supporting details (elaborates on the main points, provides evidence or proof to support assertions or opinions)
- terms (key vocabulary or concepts)
- K-W-L technique – fill out the table while tackling a subject:
  - K = background knowledge
  - W = what you would like to know about the topic
  - L = learned (read the material and note what you have learned).

Know already	Want to learn	Learned

TEN TOP TIPS

General strategies:

1. Encourage your child to seek written directions along with oral instructions if they need to – an email to a teacher if uncertain etc.
2. Help your child to be aware of and plan for transition times and shifts in activities during the day, so that they are more prepared for this as they progress through the day.

Managing time:

1. Provide visual schedules for the school week, and encourage your child to complete them, review them and refer to them several times a day. Use visual calendars to keep track of longer-term projects, due dates for tasks and for activities.
2. Promote the use of time organisers, watches with alarms, alerts etc. to remind them when to do something.
3. Encourage your child to create checklists and 'to do' lists; record due dates and estimate how long each task will take. Read all directions before attempting to start a task.
4. Encourage them to break projects into chunks and assign a time frame for completing each chunk.

Managing space and materials:

1. Encourage your child to keep a clutter-free workspace, free from distractions.
2. Schedule a weekly time for them to clean and organise the workspace.
3. Provide useful supplies, such as pencils, pens, paper, ruler, paper clips, pencil sharpener, dictionary, calculator etc. Label

drawers in the study area desk or table and help your child place supplies in the designated drawer.

Managing work:

1. Encourage them to troubleshoot problems, so that they are taking more control of their anxieties.

AND ALSO...

It is important to remember that your executive functions continue to develop until well into your twenties, so no matter what age your child or teenager is, they can still develop and hone these skills.

Chapter 4

STRUCTURE AND FLEXIBILITY WORKING IN TANDEM

In this chapter we will consider:

- how children with ADHD need structure more than anything; we will look at not just what to do but how to do it
- how flexibility can complement structure in effective and proactive strategies
- the concept of supporting mood rather than behaviour management.

They say that the most important thing when buying a house is location, location, location; when that same rule of three is applied to supporting and parenting a child with ADHD, the most important thing is structure, structure, structure.

Why would this be?

It is a complete myth that people who have differences in behaviour issues hate structure. It is actually the case that those who appear to be fighting against structure the most need it the most, and deep down they know this, though often they would be loath to admit it.

We as a society live by rules and regulations because in essence this provides safety and security. This is one of the reasons why schools have behaviour polices that provide a structure for everyone within the community to work and live together. As in all communities there are rules by which people need to abide, and although not everyone will be happy with all of the rules outlined they will mostly try to follow the expectations, at least initially.

You may be thinking that home should be different from school and from outside in the community, but home should also be an integral part of the community, especially for children with impulsive and hyperactive traits. I have many families who have an aversion to setting boundaries or rules or who say that their children can't follow these, but in essence if you want to really help and support children with ADHD then structure is vital. It provides the following:

1. reduced anxiety
2. enhanced motivation, confidence and self-esteem
3. increased concentration through reducing distractions
4. facilitation of independence.

However, as in many things it's not just what you do but the way that you do it. Let's look at the definition of 'rules', 'rituals' and 'routines':

- **Rules**: One of a set of explicit or understood regulations or principles governing conduct or procedure within a particular area of activity.
- **Ritual**: A way of behaving or a series of actions which people regularly carry out in a particular situation, because it is their custom to do so.
- **Routine**: The usual series of things that you do at a particular time.

Rules

Every group situation, when you think about it, has rules to some extent. Whether you are driving on the road or playing football in the park there are guiding expectations about how this should take place. Therefore while setting regulations or principles governing conduct or procedure at home might seem quite daunting, it has to happen in order for this group situation to work.

Trust me, children understand the need for rules, as they have experienced since birth what they can and cannot do; children with ADHD certainly require clear and achievable rules to support their traits of impulsivity, inattention and hyperactivity.

So how to start the process: here are some tips for creating family rules:

1. Think about the things that matter to you and the rest of the family.
2. Get the whole family together to discuss the rules.
3. Decide on a maximum of three at the start.
4. Make them clear and brief.
5. Make them practical to enforce.
6. Make them visual in terms of charts or diagrams and pin them up in various parts of the house.
7. Some rules should apply to everyone.

Two things are absolutely vital here: not which rules you choose – which of course will be age and stage appropriate – but when and where the discussion takes place, and that all rules are followed by all members of the household.

It is also key that these rules are non-negotiable, whatever mood or stress any members of the household are in.

Times to discuss the rules could include at mealtimes when everyone is relaxed, or mostly relaxed; however if that's not possible a discussion with your child with ADHD while driving in the car, with no eye contact or movement, is also not a bad idea.

So what rules should you choose?

Often parents say to me that they want to stop the shouting or screaming or swearing or even physical confrontations; however, we can't start with these bigger issues. Instead, follow this procedure and reducing the impact of these other areas will be achievable.

I would consider starting off with something very explicit such as no shoes on in the house, no eating upstairs and no phones allowed at the kitchen table.

Why? Because they are clear and concise and you can see quite clearly the physical evidence of whether it is happening or not.

It does not have to be these specific rules but try to establish three that are practical to enforce in your situation.

At this stage you may be thinking that I have lost my mind, so I shall tell you a story.

Some years ago when I was a new teacher at a special school in London I was tasked with reducing the levels of disruption and improving discipline. I noticed that the students didn't really act any differently in the classroom to when they were in the playground.

It occurred to me that they couldn't make the distinction between how they acted in group situations outside and inside the building.

I had to make it clear to them that expectations were different in the classroom, but talking to them and disciplining them had no effect.

So I went for a couple of simple rules: no hats – baseball or otherwise – to be worn in the building, and absolutely no chewing or eating inside the building.

None of the staff liked enforcing these rules initially, as further confrontations ensued when following through, but after a while every teacher was doing it. Discipline improved dramatically as suddenly students realised that the expectations were different, and they felt different. Safer in fact.

Let's be clear. This had nothing to do with hats or chewing – it was about structure.

As mentioned above, once the rules have been established make them visual and reinforce them with occasional reviews of how they are going.

One way of thinking about how to live with a child with ADHD in terms of rules and expectations is to think of a banding system as shown in the table below.

Band 1 is non-negotiable, whether you are ADHD, ODD, ASC (or even the BBC, MTV or OTT), whereas Band 2 areas are not seen as crimes against the state. The 'structure' of Band 1 must be balanced by the 'flexibility' of Band 2 when you have a child who is developmentally different. Having said that if you are able to establish traction in Band 1 you will find the issues in Band 2, as well as your routines and rituals, will also show significant improvement.

Band 1	Band 2
Shoes off in the house	Tidy bedroom
Food remains downstairs	Fidgeting
Meal times are for eating	Calling out and chatting
Slamming doors	No eye contact

Writing the rules down is the easy bit, however keeping to the rules will be harder. And as the song says, 'it ain't what you do, it's the way that you do it...that's what gets results'.

Routines and rituals

Children with ADHD thrive on Structure and routines and rituals provide the child with a framework to be able to refer to things or issues they may forget or need to relearn.

It's like providing a safety net for an acrobat who is walking a tightrope so even if they fall this provides both safety and security and will reduce anxiety.

In terms of establishing these, this will take time and patience but if you hold the line on the rules things will start to move in a positive direction.

Areas that you could consider for routines and rituals are the following:

- getting up
- going to bed
- mealtimes
- homework
- clearing up
- self-hygiene
- TV/computer/phone time
- ...and others.

As you can see there are a number of areas to consider, and what you choose will depend on what you see as the key areas of need.

There is a story about a famous golfer who sunk a very long putt to win a major golf championship, and when the golfer was interviewed afterwards, the interviewer asked him if he felt lucky about the putt going in. The golfer, quick as flash, remarked 'the more I practice my putting the luckier I get'. The point here is that applying the rules, routines and rituals is about practice, as well as parent style and approach. These will be the most important aspects of this process.

Parenting style

In my view your parenting style:

- affects the climate in the home
- models the behaviour that your children copy.

The beliefs that you hold determine your style of approach; over the years I have worked with many families and have found three specific parenting styles which I have classified as follows:

1. the controller
2. the friend
3. the benevolent dictator.

The controller
Attitudes:

- Children should be seen and not heard.
- Don't smile till Christmas.
- If one person gets away with it, they will all do it.
- It's a battle and I aim to win it.

Strategies:

- Tell them what to do.
- Tend to only use consequences.

This is a blunt instrument approach with no 'plan B', which is why when it doesn't work the task will often be handed over to the other parent in the house. The results will be as follows.

Outcomes:

+ poor quality relationships
+ high stress
+ learning and risk taking will be impaired.

This style is mainly about being in charge and enforcing power. It will not work for all students. The style also does not allow for children to be treated as individuals, as they are all treated in the same way. It is much more about you than them. In direct contrast on the other end of the spectrum you have the next style.

The friend
Attitudes:

+ Children need nurturing like buds on a flower.
+ Being nice and friendly means children will like you.
+ Homes are a democracy where negotiation is the key.

Strategies:

+ Asking, negotiating, pleading, followed by –
+ 'Why are you doing this?' (hurt)
+ 'How many times have we been through this?' (frustration)
+ 'I'm fed up with you' (emotional outbursts).

This individual wants to be liked by the child and believes that a caring, democratic and friendly approach will be appreciated.

You will come a cropper here as children don't want you to be their friend, they want you to be their parent. The results will often be as follows:

Outcomes:

+ Uncertainty leads to insecurity.
+ Leadership of the house is up for grabs.

The benevolent dictator

This final option is what I believe to be the best style.

Attitudes:

- A parent's job is to set boundaries.
- A child's job is to test them.
- Children should be helped to experience achievement and mistakes will be part of the journey.
- Caring means sometimes being prepared to make unpopular decisions.
- The problem is the problem, not the child.
- Fairness is not giving everybody the same, it is giving them what they need.

Strategies:

- Hold children accountable for their choices.
- Create a culture of praise that focuses on what children do well.
- Redirect children towards success.
- Apply consequences, both positive and negative, with consistency.

Outcomes:

- Children learn boundaries with dignity.
- The parent is both leader and coach in the home.

It might sound a bit severe but in reality what is needed is to own the house, and this is done by setting clear objectives for learning behaviour. Having said that, children will test you to see whether your commitment to this is real or just posturing. It is also critical that you are able to cope with the fact that the child will not always like you; however what you are after is their respect, and you get this I believe by being consistent.

It is also very important that you separate the child from the behaviour, and understand that some children need more time and possibly flexibility than others – something you now understand and appreciate having read about the developmental differences of ADHD.

Dealing with one of the core issues of ADHD in the home

While the three core symptoms of ADHD are hyperactivity, inattention and impulsivity, it often appears to be the impulsivity that parents have most difficulties with. There are no hard and fast rules for trying to support children with impulsive reactions, and no magic solutions. As with most things it is not so much a matter of 'inspiration, but perspiration', these suggestions and strategies may be worth considering.

1. Outline behavioural expectations for upcoming situations. What should non-impulsive behaviour look and sound like? What will the activity consist of? For example, at the dinner table what is the likely sequence of events and the timings? Maybe sketch out the sequence with timings so your child can see the format. Don't assume they understand what impulsivity is.

2. Work with your child to develop self-awareness about their impulsive behaviour and problem-solving skills. When you and your child are both in a relaxed mood, help your child get to know their impulsive times, how it affects them and others, and what alternative behaviours they could consider. Consider role playing situations.

3. Reward them with a preferred activity or item, for getting through a specific time period (e.g. dinner, homework) without any impulsive behaviours that disrupt the environment or are hurtful/inconsiderate to self or others.

4. Encourage your child to observe their environment to notice if they see/hear impulsive behaviours. Talk about what the impulsive individual could have done differently. Discuss the situation and alternatives.

5. Children who have more down time/unstructured time are more likely to engage in impulsive behaviours. Help your child plan their day so as to reduce boredom. Fill it with preferred activities (playing outside, video games, colouring and music) and non-preferred activities (homework, chores etc.). Less down time = fewer impulsive behaviours.

6. Exercise. Studies show that regular exercise can reduce impulsivity

and hyperactivity. You may need to experiment with a range of activities or sports that work best for your child. However do not over-stimulate them or put them at risk of hurting themselves or others. Although it may sound unusual maybe consider martial arts classes that can help children with ADHD exert control over their body movements in structured and ritualistic ways.

7. Consider aspects of diet and sleep hygiene that may improve mood and therefore self-control when frustrated, and reduce impulsive actions.

8. Try not to badger or nag your child when they are frustrated about a situation in order to avoid them lashing out. Try to remain calm and focused and deal with the issue at hand.

9. Possibly consider the option of medication if other strategies are not significantly improving matters. Medication will not cure impulsivity, but it will most often allow the child to hesitate longer to allow you to support them in making different choices.

10. Accept that you will not be able to make all impulsive behaviours go away. Some individuals will have an impulsive personality, and while you want to make behaviours more appropriate, you don't want to stop someone from being themselves. Everybody can be a little impulsive at times, and in certain situations it can be a good thing. Just keep in mind that if it is inconsiderate, hurtful or disrespectful to self or others it should be addressed.

Try to remember that impulsive actions are not pre-meditated, which is why punitive responses to behaviour do not work well. These work more effectively for pre-mediated behaviours, when an individual has stopped to think and weigh up their options. For impulsivity more positive options are more likely to distract the individual towards an alternative and hopefully a better choice.

Mood and motivation management

It's not about behaviour management – it's about management of MOOD. All of my experience has shown that this issue is crucial over all other areas. We will talk about how to deal with challenging behaviours through mood management in three key areas:

1. Your own mood.
2. The mood of others in the family, including the siblings.
3. The mood of the child with ADHD.

In psychology, a mood is an affective state. In contrast to emotions or feelings, moods are less specific, less intense and less likely to be provoked or instantiated by a particular stimulus or event. Moods are typically described as having either a positive or negative valence.

Generally speaking, any word that can be used to describe emotion can be used to describe a mood. Here are some words that are commonly used to describe mood:

- cheerful
- reflective
- gloomy
- humorous
- melancholy
- idyllic
- whimsical
- romantic
- mysterious
- ominous
- calm
- light-hearted
- hopeful
- angry
- fearful
- tense
- lonely.

The parent's mood

It is always important to consider your own mood as this is vital to determining the climate and culture of the home. When we are in a good mood, we can handle everything and anybody, but we all know that things are not this easy if our mood is low. In a bad mood, we are at risk of saying things we don't mean.

When I talk about a 'good mood', I don't necessarily mean overly enthusiastic or extremely happy (although it's always great to feel these things!). A good mood for a parent is about being calm, measured and understanding. When we fly somewhere, we are told that if the cabin depressurises we have to put on our own breathing masks before we help the children with theirs. Why? Because if the adult is able to breathe properly they can then assist the children. I would argue that it is the same with mood management.

Liz Miller in her book *Mood Mapping* (2009) has taken the issue of considering mood to a new level in terms of understanding, protecting and learning how to manage your own mood. Essentially Miller claims that anxiety, depression, calm and action are the four key moods that we exhibit. Therefore, before acting or responding in certain situations, take account of where you are in context of these four areas as this will often determine the outcome of what you say and what you do.

With regards to managing your own mood there are a number of factors which are responsible for determining how it may be at any one time:

- the physical surroundings.
- your own wellbeing.
- connection with others.
- attitude to situations.

You may want to consider which of these issues most affects your ability to stay focused and in control.

The mood of others in the family

It might seem strange to focus on the mood of the child's siblings before you get to the child with ADHD, but the mood of the siblings is also vital.

The reason for this is because, since the child with ADHD has impulsivity issues, the siblings are often more in control of their responses to situations.

This does not mean they will not get frustrated with the actions of their 'annoying brother or sister', but they do have better impulse control and as such you the parent will need to engage them in helping to not accelerate any issues. You want them to work in partnership with you on this issue.

What is in for them to do this? Well, some form of positive return or reward for their help will no doubt be appreciated.

The mood of the child with ADHD

No one solution can determine mood, and as mentioned earlier it is very much a case of the more you practice your skills in mood management the better will be the outcome, but some reminders in how to do this are as follows:

Stay calm. If you the parent are out of control, you run the risk of the child's anger escalating along with the chances of a non-productive outcome. Arguing with your child won't get you anywhere. Take homework time, for instance – an activity that can feel like a tug-of-war. Arguing simply creates 'a diversion that delays homework even longer. Always try and diffuse and don't engage. For example, 'Say, "I understand this is no fun for you", followed by silence, positive expectancy and maybe a touch on the shoulder. The wrong option here would be saying, "Stop complaining. You're dawdling over nothing".

Set limits on your own behaviour. If you're inclined to be a worried, rescuing parent, remind yourself that the more you do for your child, the less they will do for themselves. The key is to 'support, but don't get into the driver's seat'.

Set structure – but make it pressure-free. At home structure may involve options like star charts for young children and calendars and planners for older ones. Have clear rules and sensible routines, especially at mealtimes and bedtimes. Structure helps reduce disorganisation and distractibility. Pressure-free structure includes not using threats or unreasonable deadlines and punishments that contribute to hostility, fear or drama.

Use reasonable consequences for rule-breaking. In most cases I would suggest parents ask their child what the consequences should be if they break a rule. This helps children create commitments that they can actually own. In addition, create and consistently enforce positive consequences for positive behaviours and negative consequences for negative behaviours. This helps your child understand that positive behaviours result in positive consequences, and negative behaviours result in negative ones.

Expect rule-breaking, and don't take it personally. It is going to happen that your child is going to occasionally break the rules. However when your child breaks the rules, respond in a non-personalised way and don't groan or yell, 'I can't believe you did that again! Why do you do this to me?' Be respectful, consistent and matter-of-fact: the child has made the choice not to follow the rule and as a result these are the consequences.

Avoid trying to dominate a headstrong child. You may have to accept that some children will protest and talk back. Although the parent must set a limit, understand that some children will need at least some way to express their frustration, while you may still enforce reasonable standards and rules.

Understand that your child isn't misbehaving on purpose. Parents of children with ADHD often subconsciously make assumptions about why their child is misbehaving. In fact children with ADHD are very goal-directed and do what they do with the hope of obtaining an outcome they seek. This usually pertains to something they want to do or get, or something they are trying to avoid like chores, homework or bedtime.

Be persistent. Children with ADHD may require more trials and exposure to consistent consequences in order to learn from that experience. Trying a technique one or two times with no results doesn't mean that it's ineffective. You just might have to keep trying.

Tackle one issue at a time. Every concern can't be fixed at once so it's important to prioritise what situations seem most important, and start with those, temporarily letting go of the less important problems.

Educate yourself about ADHD and attention. Knowing how ADHD symptoms affect your child is essential. You might think that your child is being stubborn or behaving a certain way on purpose, but these actions may be symptoms of ADHD. The other important part is educating yourself about attention and learning when your child is at their peak of productivity.

KEY POINTS

- Supporting children with ADHD will require structure alongside flexibility, which do not contradict but rather complement each other when outlined clearly and followed consistently.
- Structure does not just mean rules and boundaries, it means devising rituals and routines for children with ADHD to live alongside parents and siblings.
- Parenting style will be crucial in terms of employing structure

and flexibility, and in the majority of cases the 'benevolent dictator' approach will be the most successful.

- Supporting mood may well be a more proactive and pragmatic approach in terms of establishing positive aspects of behaviour. Positive mood leads to motivation and provides direction for change.

AND ALSO...

Many people might say that structure and flexibility are contradictory, but in essence they are complementary; in my opinion they are the twin key pillars of supporting children with ADHD. However, as in most situations it is not what you do but how you do it, and being consistent but occasionally going off-piste is also important. Keep in mind the idea of supporting mood and not behaviour. It's all about creating a positive mood – if you don't, you get 'mood' spelt backwards. Think about it.

You need to look after yourself to look after them. In order to do this consider how best to protect your mood, and thereafter your patience thresholds. Exercise is a good method of supporting mind, body and soul. Consider how to best manage your mood effectively and remember that if they shout at you, it's usually not about you, it's about them – you just happen to be standing in the way.

Chapter 5

EFFECTIVE PARENTING, COMMUNICATION AND DEVELOPING RAPPORT

This chapter will outline how to develop:

- effective parenting strategies
- effective communication strategies
- rapport and trust.

Introduction

Often, it's not what you say but *how* you say it. This chapter will outline some handy techniques about how we communicate and develop trust with our ADHD child. We will consider a number of scenes and situations displaying the use of positive approaches both in terms of words and body language, and how using these effectively can help to diffuse and

support ADHD behaviours, which can sometimes escalate into oppositional behaviours.

Albert Mehrabian (1939) developed a 7/38/55 rule of communication
known as Mehrabian Communication Theory.

He defined communication as follows:

1. words: 7 per cent
2. tonality, volume and tempo: 38 per cent
3. non-verbal signals: 55 per cent.

This is worth remembering as we progress through this chapter, because
children are wise and savvy and can detect so much about our feelings
from our non-verbal signals and from the way we speak to them, regardless
of the words we use. In this chapter we will try to help provide strategies
so that words, signals and tone are all working in positive harmony.

Having a chapter which focuses on communication was important to
us because we know that being a parent of a child with ADHD elevates you
into superhero status, and whilst parenting can be challenging and stressful
for anyone, it can be especially so when parenting a child with ADHD. This
is because the ADHD behaviour your child displays often calls for a negative
response from you and, if persistent, can set up a negative communication
framework. In this chapter we hope to give some guidance about how to
deal with this, as well as giving strategies to help you manage your ADHD
child's relationships both inside and outside the home.

What is key to remember is that ADHD children are likely to have a
three- or four-year delay in the development of their executive function
skills (see Chapter 3), and therefore whilst you might think you are parenting a 13-year-old, some aspects of their functioning might be more
age-appropriate to a 9- or 10-year-old. And whilst this might not provide
you with instant comfort, what is important to hold in mind, particularly
in moments of high stress, is that a child's EFs continue to develop and
mature until well into their twenties, and therefore any difficulties or
tensions that feel so real in the present moment do not tend to be lifelong,
and your child *will* mature and develop – just maybe not at the rate you
expect, or at the same rate as their peers.

Whilst this knowledge might provide you with some solace, when
you are living through it, relationship tensions and emotional dysregulation are very real and can be a struggle for all involved. Without doubt,

uncontrolled emotional explosions from your ADHD child are very difficult to live with, but it is important to remember that they are not a personal attack on you, so the key is to try to depersonalise them so that it becomes easier for you to see the struggling child/teen beneath the dysregulated behaviour, rather than an attacking child/teen. We hope to give you strategies to help deal with this over the next few pages.

Look after yourself first! ...which will help you to look after your child

As strange as it might sound, one of the best things you can do to help foster shared language and effective communication and to build rapport and trust with your ADHD child is to prioritise looking after yourself! We have already identified that all parents need to be superheroes, but parenting a child with ADHD behaviours can be extremely challenging and stressful, particularly when the behaviour often calls for a negative response from parents. Therefore, parents of ADHD children may well become overwhelmed and exhausted far more quickly than parents with neurotypical children.

It is also worth observing at this point that there is often a strong genetic component attached to ADHD, and whilst many parents may not be aware of it, or may not have received a diagnosis, some may also be managing their own struggles and possibly neurodiverse traits. This will make parenting a dysregulated child even more challenging, because the adult is required to plan ahead, problem-solve, be organised, and be able to manage negative reactions and dysregulated behaviours, when they themselves might be struggling with their own difficulties in these areas. It is important to acknowledge that some parents may have difficulty managing their own emotions and may struggle with the motivation to make changes to benefit their children – and therefore looking after yourself first is key to being able to successfully manage your ADHD child.

An analogy that springs to mind in the heat of trying to manage an 'ADHD moment' with a child is the advice we are given about oxygen masks when taking a flight with young children – the flight attendant always reminds us that in the event of an emergency, if travelling with children, we need to put our own mask on first, because we have to take care of ourselves first before we can take care of our children. So, coming back to how to parent an ADHD child, looking after your own wellness and mental health is key, and if you are able to do this, it will benefit your child and the family more generally.

This is all well and good, but how, in reality, do we as parents manage to achieve this? Here are some strategies and suggestions that could – and perhaps should – become embedded into our daily lives and routines, that allow us to provide 'self-care' so that we can then care for others (and in particular, of course, care effectively for our ADHD child):

1. Become aware of, and keep track of, your own mood. Your mood will have a direct impact on those around you, including your ADHD child. There are free online mood trackers that can help you do this, or you can use pen and paper.
   - Discover what time of day works best for you to reflect and track your mood – be that first thing in the morning before the new day starts, or in the evening once the day is over. Use the time to take stock of the day that has just gone – How was it? How did you feel? How did you parent?
   - The two things are intertwined: when we are stressed, we cannot give care as effectively as when we are not, and when we are struggling to give care effectively, it will create a feeling of low mood.

2. Take time to do things you enjoy – we put our children first all the time and do not prioritise ourselves. It is easier said than done, but positive activities have a big impact on our wellbeing. They can increase our energy and improve mood. Which benefits not only us, but our family too.
   - Try to schedule these activities once or twice per week, and then continue to monitor your mood.
   - If you keep track of your response to those activities, as well as to more difficult scenarios that occur during the week, you can begin to learn more about yourself – what has a positive and negative impact on you and your moods? And you then need to work hard to keep the balance and not slip back into forgetting to prioritise your need for some 'time out'.

3. Factor smaller good activities into your life each day – these smaller things might only take a few moments out of your day but can impact mood too. Be fully present when you are doing them, rather than thinking about all the other things on your 'to do'

list – these smaller activities can include things like taking a long bath, putting time aside to read a chapter of your book and so on.

4. Use organisational tools to help you – get into the habit of using a schedule or calendar system, and if possible have it printed out and somewhere visible – children generally benefit from having a schedule or calendar system, and ADHD children function much better with one. For example, you could have a schedule about your household's bedtime routine and morning routines. It then becomes a visual, non-confrontational reminder, rather than having to verbally repeat them and 'nag' (in your child's eyes) each day.

5. It is also important for us adults to set good routines for ourselves. – e.g. you could commit to getting up half an hour earlier than your child, to give you time to think about and organise the day to help make it run more smoothly – this will then probably have a knock-on positive impact on your mood – and the mood of your child. When thinking about setting up good routines and good practice, here are some tips to bear in mind:
   - Bedtime routines are said to be as important for adults as they are for children. They help with time management, and also help to ensure that we, as adults, get sufficient sleep to function properly.
   - Set realistic expectations about what your day will look like/ what you will achieve and create a realistic list of things to do.
   - Break tasks down into manageable chunks.
   - Prioritise items on the list – order them in terms of priorities from most important to least important, and things to do eventually.
   - Remember to list and prioritise the pleasurable activities too!
   - Consider the benefits of an electronic calendar – most of us have our phones on us all the time and we can add things instantly. Therefore, we can use our phones to set recurrent appointments and reminders. We can also set alerts – this can work really well for people who hyper-focus or are forgetful.

6. Learn to relax.
   - Try not to get stressed – this often leads to big swings of emotions.
   - Try relaxation techniques – breathing, muscle relaxing, use websites, mindfulness (being present in the moment).

7. Learn new ways of thinking – and develop your metacognitive awareness (i.e. your ability to self-reflect).
   - Often if we have been cross or angry with our child, we might then become over-indulgent in other areas of their lives to try to compensate for this. Try to recognise this pattern of behaviour – and try to self-regulate to avoid the loss of temper.
   - Try not to over-compensate if you do have lapses and do become cross and angry, because this can be confusing for a child and send mixed messages to them.
   - If your thoughts, feelings and behaviours become negative they tend to negatively spiral and affect your interactions with others – so try to develop your ability to self-regulate and self-reflect.
8. Catch your child being good – praising them might also make you feel more positive...and if they respond well, it will make you feel even better about them.
   - Remember they *should* behave a certain way depending on the age and stage that they are at – and, importantly, this includes the age and stage that they are at in terms of the maturity of their EF skillset. This may require a certain readjustment of your expectations of them.

And remember, parenting is hard work, and we do not get it right a lot of the time – reframing our lapses so that we say to our child 'I shouldn't have responded like that, I know that, and I will try not to next time...' turns negative thinking around, as well as letting your child know that we all make mistakes. It also indirectly models behaviour management skills to them.

Changing our patterns of thinking and behaving takes time and effort, and they will not be transformed overnight, but they are definitely worth working on. It is difficult to manage emotions – both in ourselves and in a dysregulated ADHD child. However, if you start from a more positive position, because you have put your oxygen mask on first, it will hopefully be easier and more successful for all involved.

Developing good communication techniques
Being able to successfully communicate with your ADHD child about functional/daily issues

When you need to communicate with your child, and it isn't about building rapport, but is about getting things done and the functionality of the day, then the way you approach these conversations may make a difference to their outcome. Reframing the way we pose requests may make a difference to how they are received:

1. Let's...
2. I need you to...
3. In five minutes you will have...
4. When I return I will see...
5. Today we are going to...
6. You will be...
7. I expect you to...
8. I know that you will...
9. Thank you for...

All these openers help your child to understand what is about to happen or what you need them to do, without appearing to nag. They also make your child feel that they are part of the decision-making process because you are not issuing ultimatums. Some children, particularly the more defiant ones, respond much better to choices rather than feeling boxed in and restricted, with no alternative options – therefore for these children, wherever possible, try to offer a '...this or that' option when asking them to do something. As parents we also need to practice the art of consistency – consistency in our approach and responses. In challenging situations, we need to keep check of our emotions, and always watch our body language as well as our words.

Also, we as parents need to try to get into the habit of catching our children 'getting it right', so that daily interactions are a mix of the inevitable instructions and requests for them to do things, some light-hearted interaction, and some positive and meaningful praise. However, what is important to remember is one of the opening comments of this chapter – our children are savvy and wise, and we need to remember that we must catch them genuinely being good at something, because empty praise will soon be detected by a discerning child and will come to mean very little to them.

Your child/teenager's role in effective communication

Remember whilst it is your role to be consistent and to also say 'no' to things, it your child's job to push boundaries and test you to see how far they can push you. Consistency is key – and remember children like to know where the boundaries are, and how to operate within them So this is all normal. The main thing to remember is that if we as adults can manage the mood of the situation, then we are more likely to be able to diffuse tension and de-escalate negative reactions – this will require us as adults to also manage our own mood and not be drawn into conflict by our children. The way we frame requests will hopefully make a difference to the response we get.

So instead of saying 'Stop making so much noise', consider reframing it and being positive and specific, e.g. 'I am working. Please can you play your music in a different room' or 'Can you please use the headphones while playing video games because I still need to work?'

The responsibility that your child has is to know and understand that they are responsible for their own actions – they cannot always revert to blaming others or their ADHD for scenarios that go wrong. They need to understand that they 'own' their behaviour and need to accept responsibility for their own actions – regardless of the injustice or provocation preceding it.

Connecting with your child through conversation

This needs to be approached from a developmental point of view, i.e. what stage is your child at, not what age they are, because these can be two different things. The idea of this is to reintroduce some fun and laughter into conversations, where communicating with your child might have become more functional or perhaps more tense in its exchanges. So, instead of trying to engage them with what they will consider to be prying topics of conversation, set up opportunities to engage with them on a lighter level – for example play games of 'would you rather...' and then give them some silly options to choose from, which may open up the chat and allow you to laugh and have some fun together. Try to focus on things your child is interested in and keep it easy, light and fun.

Parent/child talk time

- Set the timer for a length of time the child is capable of holding a conversation for – consider extending it by one minute per week to build this capacity if it is not one of their strengths.
- Reduce external sounds – find a quiet place in the house, stop what you are doing and listen if the child needs to speak.
- Take time to connect with the child when their ADHD symptoms are most under control – figure out the best time of day for them.
- Empathise, empower and affirm – remember you can empathise and affirm without necessarily agreeing with what they are saying.

When your child or teenager tries to initiate conversation with you

If our child or teenager wants to talk about something important or upsetting to them, our role is to validate their feelings and create space to let them talk about what has happened. Below are some tips on how to encourage your child to talk to you about important issues:

Top tips for non-verbal positive signals:

- Engage in focused, active listening.
  - Make eye contact when possible and appropriate.
  - Give the conversation your complete focus.
  - Don't respond with a negative emotional reaction – try not to jump to conclusions and keep those emotions in check, because otherwise your body language may relay what you are thinking.
  - Try not to interrupt, and let the other person finish before you contribute.
- Consider your positioning when you talk – your height and level in relation to the other person – and consider being at their height.
- Also take into account personal space.
- Try to be calm and not fidget.
- Try to be relaxed and fully committed to the conversation – for example, nodding to show engagement.

Connections with a secondary school-aged child/teenager

When heightened hormones and emotions are in play you will need to finely hone your parenting instincts to communicate with them effectively – you will need to react to how they are presenting themselves to you and feeling in that moment. In terms of conversation openers to get your teenager chatting to you, remember it is always safer for them to answer general questions about the world – you can bring on anxiety or defensiveness if you ask them about themselves. Therefore, consider starting with general questions first. The safer questions to ask are about what's going on in the world around them – for example: 'What's the hardest thing about school?', 'What do kids want more of in school?', 'What don't kids like about school?' Keep communication open and safe about what they are seeing around them.

Deeper more personal questions

These conversations need to happen when your child/teenager feels safe, and it will probably not be when they have just come out of school, or had an argument with a family member – even though those times might be when *we* want to talk to them. The ideal time for those deeper chats is probably when you are in the safety of your home and your teenager is calm and willing to engage with you – it might follow on from the more general chat outlined in the previous section, if your teenager has engaged willingly in that...but it's unlikely to always work out this way.

The deeper kinds of questions to think about include:

- Which friends do you want to see more of?
- What's your favourite thing at school?
- What do you want to achieve (this can be in the immediate or with a longer forecast) and how can you get there?
- What is important to you about the future?
- What do you think you want to do?

After you have asked them the questions and listened you could say, 'and what else...?' to get a deeper response.

If you can train your child to engage with you in these kinds of conversations then you are beginning to act as a coach or adviser for them, and you can begin to be seen as helpful rather than having a critical voice.

Remember:

- You don't have to agree with them or their responses to be empathetic with them – and never, during these chats, come across as critical.
- Let them know how important it is to you to have had the chat.
- Don't forget the power of the non-verbal – cultivate a look of listening and being interested.

How to build connections and develop rapport – in the home

Strong family bonds can strengthen positive pro-social emotions. It is really important for us to be able to capitalise on small moments in our day when we can connect with our children in a way that extends beyond the functionalities and routines of the day and is focused purely on enjoying each other's company and when we can give them our full attention, as well as finding ways to let them take ownership of shared activities. Creating quality time for them will help our child see themselves as part of a family unit or 'team' and create a sense of belonging which is a crucial part of helping them to build their emotional brain.

During these moments we should highlight positive behaviour – 'catch them being good' – and capitalise on it by showing appreciation of the desired behaviour. We should also be encouraging independent thinking and problem-solving skills – because these skills help them learn to regulate their own emotions.

Bonding

Remember when trying to bond with your child/teenager you need to make it developmentally appropriate – and age does not always equal developmental stage.

We need to remember the delay in the development of the EFs and allow for there to be up to a 30 per cent delay for children with ADHD. Therefore, you will need to choose the most appropriate way to deal with your child/teenager based on your assessment of this.

Here are a few suggestions of ways to bond with your child which are focused on giving them the signal that you have the time and drive to spend time doing activities that they enjoy:

Activities and games

- Make sure you factor in developmental age and stage.
- Begin each activity with a purpose in mind – and remember you are trying to connect with your child/teenager, not trying to teach or discipline them.
- Listen for connections – and use the opportunity to let them talk.

Imaginary questions for bonding

- If you could go anywhere in the world, where would you go?
- If you could prevent a natural disaster which one would you prevent?
- If you could have a superpower, what would it be?

These kinds of conundrums will help your child to practice values and critical thinking but through light conversation. If you do it regularly it becomes natural and solidifies your connection with your child.

Child-led/teen-led time – it's not adult-led time!

This is about creating opportunities for your child or teen to be in control of what you jointly do together.

For child-led time – Ask them what they want to do with you for the 5/10/15 minutes etc., that you have available to devote entirely to them – allow them to choose, not you.

For teen-led time – Say to your teenager 'I have 15 minutes, what do you want to do? Watch TikTok together, YouTube?' etc. – let them choose, and fully commit to engaging with it (you may even enjoy it!). Watching and laughing at something that amuses them will help to make a connection between the two of you.

Useful things to remember include:

- Part of the process of bonding with your child is to do things with them that serve no purpose other than having fun, and are things that you can do together.
- If this is not already a habit in your household, then initially your child – and in particular your teenager – may grumble and groan at the concept of doing something with a parent, however do not

let this put you off because they will soon begin to enjoy it, and the more you do it the more they will get used to it – and the more opportunity you will have to connect with them.

- ♦ It is also important to remember that as an adult you need to put your phone away and focus on the connection with your child/ teenager, so that there are no other distractions that could send a message to them that you are not fully committed to spending this time with them.

Dealing with others: Siblings and extended family

As the parent of a child with ADHD most of us have probably been self-con-scious at some time or another of the attitude of family or friends towards our ADHD child, and most of us will probably have felt embarrassed at some point about others' perceptions of our parenting skills. We have said throughout this book that parenting a child with ADHD is not easy. One of the most difficult areas for parents and carers to deal with is explaining to others about your child having ADHD and for this not to be perceived as an excuse, but rather an explanation. Not only will we all have questioned our own parenting skills over the course of the child's life, we will also face, and continue to face, the judgement of others from time to time. There will be many a grandparent across the nation that has said words like:

- ♦ 'We never had that ADHD thing when I was growing up, it's just an excuse.'
- ♦ 'I blame the Internet and PlayStation – that's the reason for it.'
- ♦ 'All boys are busy... You just need to discipline him better.'
- ♦ 'He's just like his Dad, he has turned out right.'

Ideas for helping to the extended family to understand your child better might be as follows:

1. Manage your mood.
   As mentioned earlier, the key to how others respond (and the only thing that you have any direct control over) is your own mood – your body language and tone will give a lot away. Therefore, check in with yourself and manage your own mood, and be in the right frame of mind before tackling family!
2. Try and get the family to understand what ADHD really means.

Consider putting some information together for your extended family so that they can better understand your family dynamic. Put yourself in their shoes and think back to when you first became aware of the term ADHD and what you knew about it, and put something together for them to read and re-read, quietly in their own time, to help them catch up with all that you have learned about the condition – trying to explain it to them when they are shaking their heads in disapproval about how you just parented a situation is not the best time or way to broach their lack of understanding. This should then allow you to begin to have more open conversations with extended family – in time you may be able to encourage them to help you find workable coping strategies and problem-solve with you – but first they need to understand and take on board the concept of ADHD.

3. Pre-empt situations through effective communication.
   Once your extended family understands more about ADHD they will hopefully be open to the concept that your child is not unruly and poorly disciplined, but in fact really struggles to regulate their own emotions. Reminding family members about this before family gatherings or big family events may avoid any potential stressors during the event itself, because they will be more understanding and tolerant, and have more patience and flexibility in any highly charged scenario.

4. Give your child some agency.
   It's all well and good educating your extended family so that they are more tolerant towards your child, but your child also needs to begin to understand the impact that they might have too – it will require good timing and a thoughtful choice of words, but have a conversation with your child before a family event, so that you can remind them about the expectations and agree a signal for time-out if your child gets over-excited or upset. Being able to enlist the help of a family member for time-out would make this easier!

Non-ADHD siblings

Having an ADHD brother or sister can be quite challenging for everyone in the family, but what about the impact on a sibling who does not have ADHD and what can we as parents do to recognise this and make life at home easier?

These children may spend a fair amount of their home-time feeling frustrated, confused and exhausted by the behaviour displayed by their ADHD sibling. They may not get their 'fair' share of attention because their sibling dominates this in one way or another, which may trigger feelings of jealousy and sibling rivalry – or a sense of detachment from the family unit that has the ADHD child at its centre. There is also the thorny issue of 'fairness' – that the ADHD child might be perceived to 'get away' with behaviours that the neurotypical child gets pulled up on, or the ADHD child receives more rewards for behaviours that the neurotypical child does not. Some siblings may react in another way and take on too much responsibility within the household to compensate for their sibling – taking on the mantle of being the 'good child', which is not necessarily healthy for normal family dynamics. In any of these scenarios, as the child matures and develops, they may pull away from the nucleus of the family and feel invisible, unrecognised and less important.

So, how can we as parents try to protect against this and create as balanced a family life as possible?

Here are some suggestions about how to redress the balance and try to give affirmative and inclusive signals to the non-ADHD sibling:

- Make sure you make time for your non-ADHD child, so they are getting the positive attention they need – one way to do this is for you to set yourself weekly phone reminders, or to regularly schedule/put some time aside to spend with your non-ADHD child.
- Encourage open discussion with your child so that they feel heard – and empathise and show understanding about how hard things can be for them at times.
- Just like we as parents need to develop techniques and coping strategies, so does your non-ADHD child, so help them to develop some ways to cope.
- The boundaries that will benefit your ADHD child will also benefit your non-ADHD child, because they will provide a clear framework within which the family is working – but the key will be to ensure you operate within the boundaries and pull up transgressions.

Your ADHD child and bullying
When your child is the victim

One of the overriding concerns for parents of children with ADHD is their socialisation skills and ability to make and retain friendships. Indeed, a lot of children with ADHD end up getting bullied at some stage in their childhood or adolescence because of their ADHD traits and characteristics – their impulsivity and hyperactivity can present them with social challenges which make them easy targets. As many of us will already know, this can be both heart-breaking and frustrating as a parent, because it is really tough when our child is not included in groups activities, events or parties, but also as the parent, we feel quite powerless to resolve this issue – when our child leaves the house in the morning to go to school, we are unable to help regulate how they behave and interact, and also we are not there to resolve any issues.

Alan Train, in his book *The Bullying Problem* (1995), identified what he believed were the characteristics of those who are likely to be bullied, and more specifically those likely to be the passive victims, and those prone to be provocative victims.

These are listed as follows:

Passive victims:

1. They have a high level of anxiety and insecurity.
2. They are cautious, sensitive and quiet.
3. They have low self-esteem.
4. They have few friends.
5. They have a negative attitude towards violence.

Provocative victims:

1. When attacked by the bully they try to retaliate.
2. They may try to attack other children weaker that themselves.
3. They could be described as hyperactive as they are restless and unable to concentrate.
4. They may be clumsy and immature.
5. They may be disliked by others, including teachers, because they irritate and create tension.

If you consider these two lists you may see that the characteristics of passive victims may match those of individuals with inattentive ADHD whilst those of provocative victims match those of hyperactive impulsive ADHD.

This of course does not mean that all children with ADHD will be bullied, but the risk could well be higher.

One thing we will all be able to recall from our own childhoods is that some children can be mean – they tend to pick on others who do not fit in or conform, and so the ADHD child can become an easy victim. You cannot make children be friends with each other – no matter how hard you as a parent might try to facilitate it – therefore the best we can do is to help our child to understand those unspoken rules of social engagement.

When your child is the bully

Our ADHD children may not realise when they cross the line between teasing and ribbing people (which is done with humour and does not negatively impact self-esteem) and taunting or bullying them – they may not realise this because they are not reading the room or reactions properly. They face greater challenges interpreting body language and detecting the subtleties in conversation that might give them the cue that they need to stop their ribbing.

Sometimes children with ADHD can get drawn into becoming bullies inadvertently through their desire to fit in and increase their social standing and acceptability. They can also perhaps be more prone to responding to peer pressure, or indeed responding to negative attitudes towards them as a defence mechanism, than their neurotypical peers.

Managing anxiety and stress

If your child is anxious or upset the following strategies might be helpful:

- Do not accommodate the anxiety by giving in to the child.
- Do not get angry – be empathetic and talk about what is making them feel anxious.
- Reinforce valiant/brave behaviours with praise.
- Do not make them feel singled out or different within the family unit.
- Teach relaxation and mindfulness strategies.

When upset or stressed, stress hormones are released into the body and all the blood rushes out of the rational/thinking/calming part of the brain into the motor cortex, preparing the body for fight, flight or freeze. The emotional brain automatically takes over at this point – so talking, scolding or punishing here is pointless.

TEN TOP TIPS

In most scenarios – whether your child is a victim of taunting or bullying, being drawn into bullying behaviours or just struggling socially, the following tips may help:

1. Try to encourage your child to 'join in' with clubs and societies being offered at school and college – this provides a ready group of like-minded people with whom to make connections.

2. Try to help your child to understand that interrupting conversations and not being able to wait their turn will be irritating to others and may alienate them – you will need to pick up on this a lot at home, so that your child learns through observation and practice how to improve.

3. Develop your child's awareness that some children will try to wind them up, simply because they know that they have ADHD – the more aware of this your child is the better, because they will need to learn that they must not lash out in response, because it will be your child who gets into trouble and not the child who wound them up. The sooner they can learn this the better – and even so, we know that because of their difficulties with impulse control, they will sometimes lash out still – and we as parents need to be understanding of this and continue to work with them to improve their response inhibition.

4. The more that you can help your child to develop self-awareness and conform to the school rules the better – we have little control over this once the child is actually at school, but we can do a lot to help before they leave the house in the morning.

Helping them to be as organised as possible, so that they go to school in the correct uniform, with the correct kit that they need for that day, will help prevent them being a negative object of focus once at school.

5. Remind your child that they are not alone and have good friends (hopefully they do!). Help your child to promote and consolidate the friendships that they do have - invite children over, and help your child to develop a system whereby they know where and when to meet, if they are meeting somewhere else - you do not want your child to be the one who turns up late, and the others have already left, or to be the one who begins to get left out of plans because arrangements go wrong when they are involved.

6. Instil in your child an understanding that they need to make sensible choices and avoid getting drawn into foolish situations because they appeared 'fun' or wanted to go along with the crowd - they cannot blame risky or dangerous behaviour on their ADHD, and they run the risk of getting into trouble and, at its worst, they risk being excluded.

7. If you are aware that your child is being bullied or teased at school, do not ignore it and hope it will sort itself out - as a starting point you should contact the school's SENDCo (Special Educational Needs and Disabilities Coordinator - every school will have someone in this kind of role, whether called a SENDCo or something else). This is the person responsible for your child's additional needs and is a good point of contact to have open, or more confidential, conversations with about how to support your child. The school will also have a behaviour and bullying policy which you could ask to see, to see what steps they should take to help your child. You may wish to liaise with the SENDCo about how overtly or discreetly bullying behaviour should be addressed initially - but certainly try not to ignore it and hope it will go away!

8. If your child needs to take medication whilst at school, liaise with the school nurse who will be the one to administer it, and request that the arrangements put in place with your child can be discreet - you do not want your child being publicly reminded

that they need to go and take their medication, because this will single them out, and may make them a focus for negative attention.

9. In class try to encourage your child to recognise what works best for them, and then liaise with school to make sure these measures are in place. If your child constantly disrupts class, then they are likely to become unpopular with some – however if placing them near the teacher (and yes, that might mean away from their friends for the duration of the class) helps them to focus and attend, then that is what the teacher should do.

10. Encourage your child to observe their environment to notice any impulsive behaviours in others; this can then trigger a talk between you about what the individual could have done differently. By discussing the situation and the alternative ways it could have been handled your child is learning metacognition – how to self-reflect on their own behaviours when they hit a tricky patch. They will also realise that they are not the only ones who have these traits and characteristics!

AND ALSO...

Remember how great your child is, and that your parenting skills will be helping them to develop into more metacognitive, self-aware individuals - and remind yourself, when you need to, that they will be liked for who they are and will develop true friendships (it just will not be with everyone, and it may need some help from you from time to time).

Chapter 6

WORKING WITH SCHOOLS

This chapter will offer advice to parents on how to work in partnership with schools in dealing with a range of issues, including:

- consistent behaviour management approaches
- organisation
- homework.

Having been both a headteacher for a number of years and a consultant on behalf of parents I will in this chapter reveal the secrets of how to get the school's attention, but also what schools are looking for from parents.

Children are in school for about 12 per cent of the year – and at home hopefully sleeping for the rest of the time – so working together in an effective partnership is crucial for the child with ADHD.

Maintaining a consistent approach towards a child's behaviour at home and at school can help the parents/carers and teachers to develop a better understanding of the strengths and challenges associated with a child's behaviour. It can also prove to the child that teachers and parents talk to each other, and that there is a 'united front' in terms of agreement on important rules and expectations.

Some common approaches to managing a child's behaviour that can work at home and at school can include the following:

- **Being consistent.** This can help a child to understand that the same expectations regarding behaviour apply to both home and school.
- **Reinforcing positive behaviour.** Positive feedback for good behaviour at home or school, no matter how small the action may be, can encourage a child to repeat the behaviour as well as improve their self-esteem.
- **Providing clear consequences for bad behaviour.** Consequences for bad behaviour should be consistent and relevant to the situation, as well as communicated clearly so that a child understands the implications of their actions.
- **Acting immediately.** Both good and bad behaviour needs to be acted on as soon as it occurs so that a child can make a clear link between the behaviour and the reaction from the teacher or parent/carer.
- **Giving feedback.** Frequent feedback on all aspects of a child's behaviour can help them to understand positive and negative consequences and exactly what they have done to elicit the reaction.
- **Ensuring repetition.** Children with ADHD need repetition to help reinforce the consequences of good and bad behaviour, and this can be more effective when done both at school and at home.
- **Changing rewards and consequences as needed.** Be flexible and change the rewards and consequences for behaviour over time to help stimulate the child and prevent situations becoming predictable.
- **Keeping going.** It may take some time to change certain aspects of a child's behaviour either at home or at school so keep persisting for a long-term change in behaviour.

Common approaches to managing the child's behaviour can work more effectively if there is a strong and positive relationship between the parents/carers and the school with regular feedback from both parties. This can help both the parents/carers and school to:

- share what is and isn't working successfully
- set and re-set behaviour targets for the child as appropriate
- ensure greater consistency of approach for a greater response
- build a stronger relationship.

Feedback can also be improved by:

- agreeing the method of communication that works best for the parent/carer and teacher, e.g. telephone, text, email, face-to-face meeting
- agreeing how regular the feedback should be and under what circumstances
- teachers letting the parents know when positive as well as challenging behaviour occurs; this can help to build a more productive relationship between the parents/carers and teacher
- sharing new approaches that have produced positive results.

It is also a good idea to think about creating a plan or a discussion guide to support a positive and proactive meeting between parents/carers and teachers to agree a consistent approach to managing behaviour at home and at school.

There will obviously be individual and joint targets for parents/carers and teachers, but it is prudent to set out some areas for discussion in advance.

Below I have listed some suggestions for both teachers and parents to consider for a proactive meeting:

For teachers:

- What you consider to be the priorities for good behaviour by the specific child.
- How you could manage the expectations of the parents/carers in terms of improving the child's behaviour consistently over time.
- Behaviour targets that could be agreed with the child's parents.

- How often you could provide feedback to the parents/carers and when is appropriate.
- Are there particular areas of the child's behaviour that should be focused on, based on how the child behaves at home?
- When attending a previous school, did the child behave very differently at home and at school?
- What are the parents' main challenges in terms of managing the child's behaviour at home?
- What have been the main areas of focus for previous teachers in managing the child's behaviour?

For parents:

- Your expectations of the school in maintaining a consistent approach to managing your child's behaviour.
- The priorities for maintaining a consistent approach to managing your child's behaviour.
- How often you would like to receive feedback on your child's behaviour from the school.
- Information you could provide to help agree a consistent approach with the school.
- How you successfully manage good and challenging behaviour at home and how this might apply in school.

Also you may want to consider listing questions that you want to discuss at the meeting, for example:

- What common approaches can be agreed with the school in terms of managing your child's behaviour?
- Has the school any experience of working with other parents/carers to maintain a consistent approach to managing a child with ADHD's behaviour?
- What does the school consider the most challenging aspects of maintaining a consistent approach between home and school environments?
- What information could be provided to help maintain a consistent approach?

- How often can feedback on your child's behaviour take place and what is the best way to communicate?
- How can the school reassure you that it will aim to maintain a consistent approach between home and school?
- Can you set joint behaviour targets?

Finally it will be important to agree who will do what action, by when:

- Agree what the teacher and parents will do, e.g. provide further information that can help the school.
- Agree a timeline for these actions to be carried out.
- Agree when the common approach to managing behaviour between home and school will start.
- Agree who will produce a summary of the meeting with action points.

They say it takes a village to raise a child. That it is certainly the case in teaching, managing and parenting a child with ADHD.

It will not always be easy but it is certainly not impossible, as long as schools and parents/carers develop effective communication systems and are working in partnership on behalf of the child or adolescent with ADHD.

Maybe both you and the children may universally dread it, but for a parent of a child with ADHD, homework is not only a challenge but an opportunity. Academic work done outside the classroom provides you as the parent with a chance to directly support your child. It's a time you can help your child succeed at school where you both feel most comfortable: your own living room.

With your support, your child with ADHD can use homework time not only for subject work but also to practise the organisational and study skills they need in the classroom. This won't work for all families, however, which is why you will need to have a number of flexible approaches, such as those listed below.

TEN TOP TIPS

There is a fairly established statistic that it takes a child with ADHD three times as long to do the same assignment in the home environment in comparison with the school setting.

With this in mind it is recommended that the following options should be considered for children with ADHD with regards to homework:

1. Can homework be reduced to that which is essential? Is the homework really necessary, and if so can the amount or style be adapted for the child with ADHD? Perhaps more one-word answers than essays or multiple choice answers for maths.

2. Can bonus points be provided for doing more? In some cases it will be necessary to have extended assignments and in this case can the school provide extra incentives for a child with ADHD to complete the task? This arrangement can help to provide additional focus on the task.

3. Could there be ways of reducing writing requirements, e.g. dictation onto tape recorder or computer use. Writing tends to be a difficult skill for many children with ADHD. As a result providing another option for getting thoughts onto a hard copy will be necessary. As a result encourage the use of technology to assist the homework process.

4. Can students stay at school to finish homework or complete it during the day? Based on the above statistic it may be more productive to have the child complete homework tasks at school where there will be more structure and fewer distractions.

5. Can parents be allowed to be a 'parent secretary' for students with handwriting difficulties? In some cases technology will not be appropriate, and so if writing is a problem then look to use the parent as a scribe to write down the thoughts of the child (but obviously not to do the work for them).

6. Develop a place in the home that is distraction-free. This does not mean therefore that bedrooms are always the best place to

study. Depending on the rooms available it is advisable to have a place without clutter or people passing through.

7. In contrast to point 6 can you create proactive distractions if distraction-free is not available? This may mean a child can listen to music on their headphones in order to filter out other distractions.

8. Allow movement options. Children with ADHD will require structured movement when studying so providing breaks and hand manipulatives or doodle pads will be necessary. The obvious danger is too much use of alternatives will diminish the homework outcome, so some degree of supervision will be necessary.

9. Consider food and drink options. This does not mean just hydration for the child but what time of the evening is best for the child to complete homework. Possibly it is better to have a snack prior to homework and the main meal after, however this will depend on the patterns of each family.

10. Communication of the due dates and of the specific homework assignments is crucial between school, the child and the home. How is this going to take place and by which electronic means? All parties need to be clear on this issue.

AND ALSO...

Homework is supposed to support curriculum objectives during the school day and in my opinion as a former teacher and headteacher we should try to take the burden of homework away from parents and carers if it is problematic. For the family of a child with ADHD who are trying to manage a range of issues on a school night to enforce homework on a reluctant child can be a bridge too far, and alternative options should be considered.

Choosing a school

One of the questions I am often asked is about what type of school is most appropriate for children with ADHD, and that I'm afraid is a very difficult question.

The key issue is that a parent needs to consider whether the school can meet and support the academic, behavioural and socialisation needs of their child.

It is unfortunate that many schools do not have staff who are trained in a range of SEND issues including ADHD and do not have the systems in place to support non-traditional learners.

As a parent you should be completely aware about the school policies on behaviour, SEND and anti-bullying policies, and ask specific questions in advance regarding potential situations that may impact on your child.

In addition you may also want to find out what the school's attitude is towards penalising or supporting difficulties in organisation.

Whenever I provide training for schools, I use the phrase: 'Fairness is not giving everybody the same – it is giving them what they need.'

During these sessions, one of the questions I am regularly asked, particularly at secondary schools, is about disorganisation and ADHD. Often in the discussion some staff feel that punishment is the best method of changing the outcome for specific students. They believe that by making any exceptions, the teacher would be letting a student get away with the behaviour and that they would never learn to take responsibility. Some point out that the other students would deem this to be unfair.

It is at this point that I tell the story of Nathan:

Nathan was a bright but extremely disorganised 14-year-old with ADHD who seldom had a pen in his possession when he arrived to my 11:20 Science class. He may have started out the day with one in the morning lessons, but by the time he came to my class after the morning break, he was pen-less.

This had been extremely annoying. I had tried everything. I had started with discipline by giving him detentions for lack of organisation as well as positives such as merits when he brought in his equipment. However, there was never any consistency with the issue. It was extremely frustrating that nothing worked.

On one particular day when I must admit I was not in the best mood, I asked the students to start working on a written assignment and up went Nathan's hand straight away.

'Can I borrow a pen Sir?'

Infuriated, I replied, 'Nathan what have a told you before about not bringing a pen to class? You never bring a pen.'

'No that's not right Sir', he said. 'I had one on Tuesday – do you remember? You said well done.' He sat there with a huge grin on his face waiting for my reply.

'Well you haven't got one today and you don't seem to care.' I snapped back.

'I do care Sir', he said sheepishly. 'I think I lost it in Maths.' He then added, 'Maybe it's at the bottom of my bag.'

With this he tipped his bag upside down and all his files and books fell out. In addition, a whole multitude of other items tumbled onto the desk. After the impact of shaking the bag, his lunch box had opened and out came his tuna sandwich, a collection of little raw carrots and his yoghurt carton – now damaged and leaking. The chaos made all of the students around him laugh.

I was furious and shouted at him, 'Nathan clear up this mess right now. Why won't you ever bring a pen to my class?'

Nathan, practically in tears, yelled back at me, 'Why don't you keep one for me?'

I was initially shocked and was taken aback for two reasons:

1. I didn't want to look as if I was giving in on this issue in front of the rest of the class.
2. It really wasn't such a bad idea.

From that day forward I kept a pen in my desk for him. He borrowed it at the start of the lesson and gave it back to me at the end.

He was happier, I was happier, and you know who was happiest of all? The rest of class! When Nathan dragged me into a negative mood and mindset the other students had to endure this for the rest of the lesson. This was a win–win for everyone.

This still raises the question: is this fair? Particularly to the other students? Will they not take advantage of the situation and expect the same treatment? The key is that **'fairness isn't giving everybody the same – it's giving everybody what they need'.**

Nathan often came to class with shoes on the wrong feet and looked world weary at the age of 14, despite being a fun and quirky individual. Although he was intelligent, he was so badly organised that I started to realise that for him, getting to class on time with his bag still intact was as much as he could achieve at that time. Remembering his pen was just a bridge too far.

This then allows me to explain to the staff at the training that children with ADHD are developmentally different from their peers, and actually the other students recognise this, but they don't always know why. The result, in the case of Nathan, was that the rest of class completely accepted the strategy I had devised. Furthermore, they still all brought their pens to class and didn't have a problem with how I managed him. They knew he was different and required an alternative approach.

Having said that, as a thank you to the 'pen bringers' we had a raffle ticket draw every week and a chocolate bar was awarded. Nathan never won that chocolate bar but he didn't mind because he didn't get told off and was able to keep his lunch intact. He was happy with the solution, as were his peers.

To be honest it's rare that all the staff in the training session agree with this approach – but a lot more will than did before the session.

As a parent in choosing a school you will have to consider carefully that the school can meet the needs of your child with ADHD; here is a checklist of some key points to help in this process.

School checklist:

1. Do the staff understand the concept of neurodiversity and have they been trained in this area or is training on this planned?
2. Do the school's behaviour and anti-bullying policies take into account point 1?
3. Does the school understand the issues of developmental differences within the term ADHD?
4. Does the school understand that ADHD is a neurodevelopmental condition as described in the NICE guidelines?
5. Have adequate provisions been made in both classroom and non-structured time in terms of supporting impulsivity and inattention issues for students with ADHD?
6. What arrangements are in place to monitor medication if required by students with ADHD?
7. Are there flexible approaches to issues such as organisation and homework for students with ADHD?
8. What communication processes are in place for working in partnership with the parents of students with ADHD?
9. Are special arrangements allowed in tests and exams for students with ADHD?
10. Are mentoring and/or counselling options available for students with ADHD?

This essentially is making the point that parents need to choose a school which not only understands the condition of ADHD and what that means in terms of the differences in learning, behaviour and socialisation, but which also embraces these differences.

Something I always say to parents is, 'Never consider whether your child is deserving of the school, but is the school deserving of your child?'

Obviously there are a number of other factors in choosing a school in terms of family location and, if there are siblings, whether you can logistically get all the family members where they need to go every day.

Though easier said than done, it is a vital decision that may be crucial in providing your child with a platform for success.

The decision on a specialist school over a more traditional school will be based on the specific level of needs of the child, and regions will differ in terms of the level of choice.

It is difficult to find what you might call ADHD-friendly schools, but perhaps parents should ask whether the staff at the school have had training on ADHD and what the approach to neurodiversity is throughout the school in terms of learning, behaviour and socialisation amongst the students.

I know as a former headteacher of an independent specialist school that when I asked parents why they chose our school they often said that they trusted me and they had a gut feel or instinct that the school was right for them. As a headteacher you will recruit and retain staff members who you recognise have the same values and skills in teaching and supporting children that you do. This means that if you trust the headteacher, you can usually also put your trust in the staff that they lead.

One more recommendation is to join a local parent ADHD forum or group where local knowledge about suitable schools will be most accurate from the very people experiencing the situation: families themselves.

Finally there a register for schools which provide support for children with dyslexia and neurodivergence called CReSTeD (www.crested.org.uk).

KEY POINTS

- Working in partnership with schools is absolutely crucial and the key issue will always be communication between home and school and developing positive and proactive relationships with the child's main advocate at the school.
- Sensible options in supporting issues such as organisation and homework need to be considered for children with developmental differences, and agreed practices and reactions to be considered between school and home prior to incidents occurring.
- Choosing a school for a child with ADHD will involve a number of factors: the level of support must be measured primarily in terms of attitude and commitment among the head and senior staff at the school in supporting children with ADHD.

AND ALSO...

You as the parent will have to trust your instincts that the school you choose for your child will value them as much as you do.

Chapter 7

MEDICATION AND OTHER FACTORS TO CONSIDER IN SUPPORTING YOUR CHILD WITH ADHD

In this chapter we will:

- consider the issue of medication in supporting children with ADHD
- outline the main categories of medication available and the process and support for application and monitoring
- outline how nutrition, exercise and sleep can impact on ADHD symptoms, and some tips and resources for support.

One of the most difficult decisions for parents to take in relation to supporting their children with ADHD is whether, after a recommendation has been made by a clinician, is whether a child should consider a trial on medication.

This recommendation will usually be made after a full diagnostic assessment and a determination of level of need.

I have seen and watched many parents agonise over this issue more often than not in terms of weighing up the risks vs the benefits.

This situation has not been helped by an often extremely uninformed media regarding ADHD and medication, along with misinformation on social media platforms.

In the NICE guidelines published in 2018 the following is outlined

All medication for ADHD should only be initiated by a healthcare professional with training and expertise in diagnosing and managing ADHD.

Healthcare professionals initiating medication for ADHD should:

- be familiar with the pharmacokinetic profiles of all the short- and long-acting preparations available for ADHD
- ensure that treatment is tailored effectively to the individual needs of the child, young person or adult
- take account of variations in bioavailability or pharmacokinetic profiles of different preparations to avoid reduced effect or excessive adverse effects.

NICE (2018)

'Pharmacokinetic' means the activity of drugs in the body over a period of time considering the processes by which drugs are absorbed, distributed in the body, localised in the tissues and are then excreted.

'Bioavailability' essentially means the amount of a drug or other substance which enters the circulation system when introduced into the body and which will be able to have an active effect.

It is not the purpose of this chapter to either promote or negate the option of medication but to inform parents of the options available.

In all cases parents should be advised as outlined above by a fully trained healthcare professional, but it is prudent to be aware of some of the options that do exist.

There are two main kinds of medication options for treatment of ADHD, which can be classified as follows:

- Stimulants: methylphenidate, dexamphetamine, lisdexamfetamine – these three are actually very much alike.
- Non-stimulants: atomoxetine and guanfacine – these two are very different from the stimulants and from each other.

There may be other medication options which are sometimes considered in the treatment and management of ADHD with overlapping co-morbidities, including clonidine, risperidone, aripiprazole, melatonin and some types of antidepressants, but this will usually be discussed at a later stage of the treatment if necessary.

A full comprehensive guide to all the medicines available for treatment of ADHD can be found in the book *The Parents' Guide to ADHD Medicines* by my colleague Professor Peter Hill (2021); however, here is a list of the main ones here in the UK:

Stimulants:

Brand names for methylphenidate are: Medikinet, Medikinet XL, Equasym, Equasym XL, Ritalin, Rialin XL Delmosart, Xaggitin, Tranquilyn (exists only as short-acting immediate-release tablets), Concerta (only Ritalin, Equasym and Medikinet exist in both immediate- and extended-release forms).
Brand name for lisdexamfetamine is Elvanse.
Brand names for dexamfetamine are: Amfexa, Dexedrine.

Non-stimulants:

Brand name for atomoxetine is Strattera.
Brand name for guanfacine is Intuniv.

In terms of what they do stimulants increase the levels of a chemical messenger, dopamine, in the brain; this appears to reduce hyperactivity and impulsivity and promote attentiveness. Methylphenidate is by far the most used stimulant option and exists in both short-acting forms lasting up to 3–4 hours and long-acting forms (Concerta XL, Equasym

XL and Medikinet XL, Xaggitin XL, Ritalin XL, Delmosart) which last for extended periods during the day (although this may significantly vary from one person to another). Possible side effects of methylphenidate can include loss of appetite (this is quite common), inability to sleep and nervousness. Sometimes headaches and stomach pains can also occur. These side effects, should they be present, usually disappear as soon as medication wears off.

Monitoring both the effect of the medication in addressing behaviour and any potential side effects will always need full cooperation between parents, health professionals and others involved with the child, particularly teachers.

Non-stimulants work differently from stimulants as they increase the level of the chemical messenger noradrenalin (a natural chemical in the brain). This can help to address ADHD symptoms for some. Response to non-stimulants is usually within two weeks (although it can take more time with Strattera, as dosage is slowly and progressively increased) but maximum effect may not occur until after 6–8 weeks (especially with Strattera). Benefits include a positive effect on mood and sleep, with a reduction in anxiety. Side effects can include a lack of appetite and tummy aches. As guanfacine tends to reduce blood pressure, low blood pressure is a possible side effect (to be monitored), as well as tiredness. It shouldn't be stopped from one day to the next, as this might cause a sudden increase in blood pressure.

Teachers and support professionals should be aware that although medication is sometimes a very effective option, it is only one of the tools available in the management of ADHD. It does not 'cure' children of ADHD but simply may enable them to concentrate and learn more effectively.

I always explain to parents that 'if they couldn't play the guitar before they took medication they still won't be able to play the guitar afterwards, but it might help someone teach them how to play the guitar'. Medication may improve their focus so that someone else can teach them more effectively.

In my experience very few children with ADHD will actually enjoy taking medication, even though it may be helping them academically, behaviourally and socially. Some students do not like to feel different and they can also be embarrassed by other people (especially peers) knowing that they take medicine. In addition, a minority of students may suffer from minor side effects such as stomach upsets, especially in the early stages of treatment.

The best way of handling these issues is for the child to meet with the supervising specialist, usually a paediatrician or psychiatrist, to review the situation and discuss the options. Ideally, the child or adolescent should be positive about trying this course of action. In addition, the decision about whether or not to prescribe medication will also depend on a judgement of benefits vs the costs. Once a course of treatment is in progress, any side effects can usually be eradicated by minor changes in dosage, a change of medication or by changing the time the pills are administered.

For any child on medication, the communication between the family, the healthcare professional and the school will be crucial. However, it is also really important to emphasise that the child should be seen as the central person in this situation. The more they understand the treatment, the more likely they will be committed to it, and therefore the more probable it is that the treatment will help.

Although the decision as to whether or not medication is prescribed rests with the healthcare professional, the role of the family working with the SENDCo (or school lead SEND equivalent) is crucial in monitoring successful outcomes and reassuring the child about confidentiality within the school context.

Parents may well discuss the option of medication for their child before considering approaching a clinician. Review meetings are often the occasions when the subject comes up.

In terms of a checklist for this type of meeting the guidelines below may prove useful in preliminary discussions.

The meeting should take place only after comprehensive evaluation and in circumstances where:

- earnest attempts at non-medical interventions have proved insufficient
- the child is at risk of emotional and/or academic failure
- a child is at significant risk of harming himself or others.

Thereafter the process should be the following:

- Observations are made by teachers and parents; information is passed to the educational psychologist/clinician.

- Assessment and diagnosis are undertaken.
- A structured learning environment has already been provided and is in place.
- Regular monitoring is already taking place on performance.
- The decision is made to seek medication.
- A base rate is established (to understand exactly which dosage and which specific medication is suitable for the child) along with a clear care plan.
- A trial of medication occurs.
- Any side effects are reported and necessary adjustments are made, including monitoring weight, blood pressure, heart rate, height.
- Benefits vs disadvantages are presented and discussed with the child without putting any pressure on them.
- The situation is evaluated: regular reviews will be necessary to establish how maturation may affect the dose required and to measure all other indicators of normal health, as well as any side effects of the medication.

A key question for every family is what medication can do for their child. The answer is that it can:

- enhance attention
- improve self-control
- reduce excessive/inappropriate activity
- improve academic performance
- improve handwriting
- improve motivation.

It is also important to outline the following points (and dispel certain myths):

- Medication, while it needs to be handled wisely, can be administered safely and effectively.
- Medication does not make children into 'zombies' or stunt their growth.
- Stimulants are non-addictive and do not produce a 'high'.
- Medication should always be considered in a child with significant ADHD.

- Fine-tuning of dosage both in terms of quantity and timing is essential for effective management.
- Combinations of medications are sometimes necessary in complex cases.
- Trial and observation should be made in a number of different situations at home and in school and therefore medication during this trial should usually be taken on a daily basis.

Teachers should be fully aware of the medical trial, looking out for and reporting side effects and reporting changes over time. Any signs of tics, withdrawal, odd behaviour or poor health should be reported immediately even if the teacher is unsure about the problem or is worried about being wrong.

Also teachers should be aware that for example although a child could be on a long-acting methylphenidate, different formulations might be more effective at different ages and stages.

Navigating the medication process

ADHD is a medical and neurobiological condition, and as a result one of the options available to support the symptoms is medication, as we have discussed. Many children with ADHD do not need to take medication, however for parents considering this option, here are some suggestions regarding how to navigate this process:

1. **Learn about the prescribed medication.** Find out everything you can about the ADHD medication your child is taking, including potential side effects, how often to take it, special warnings, and other substances that should be avoided, such as over-the-counter cold medication.
2. **Be patient.** Finding the right medication and dose is a trial-and-error process. It will take some experimenting, as well as open, honest communication with your doctor. Give it a chance, and take advantage of this trial to learn about the key issues that affect you, and to take that habit of discussing and sharing ideas about ADHD and life.
3. **Start small.** It's always best to start with a low dose and work up from there. The goal is to find the lowest possible dose that

relieves you or your child's symptoms. Having said that it might also be that increasing the dosage from time to time due to the child growing up, metabolism changing etc. will be a necessity to maintain dosage efficiency.

4. **Monitor the drug's effects.** Pay close attention to the effect the medication is having on your child's emotions and behaviour. Keep track of any side effects and monitor how well the medication is working to reduce symptoms.

5. **Taper off slowly.** If your child wants to stop taking medication, call the doctor for guidance on gradually decreasing the dose. Although there is no medical risk with stimulants, abruptly stopping medication should be avoided if possible as this can lead to unpleasant withdrawal symptoms such as irritability, fatigue, depression and headaches.

6. **Don't believe everything you read.** Some reports on medication regarding ADHD are simply not accurate, so be sure to get information from professionals who know what they are talking about.

7. **Ask about the options.** There are a range of medications available for the treatment of ADHD symptoms. Some are stimulants and some are non-stimulants – be informed of the options available.

8. **Do not be influenced by people** who have negative views on medication. That is not to say do not do your own research, but unfortunately there are some people who take the view that medication should never be considered. Do what you think is best for your child.

9. **Try to involve your child in the process.** Obviously this will depend on the age and stage of the child but it is a good idea to explain to them why they may need to take the medication to help support them at home and at school.

10. **You are in control of the situation.** If medication is not right for your child then consider alternatives as you are the guardian of your child.

Medication is a choice that each family may consider in supporting children with ADHD. If you believe the symptoms are a result of neurobiological differences then considering medication to support your child is a viable option. If you believe the symptoms are the result of a poor diet, computer games or a range of environmental factors then I understand why some people would have a different opinion.

Alongside the issue of medication of course is the question of how the lifestyle of the child can be supported in terms of nutrition, sleep and exercise.

Let's take a look at each of these in turn.

Nutrition and ADHD

When I was a science teacher teaching Biology on the topic of Nutrition I remember most textbooks would talk about the dangers of excess sugars, and carbonated drinks being one of the major causes of hyperactivity. The facts are that there is no clear scientific evidence that ADHD is caused by diet or nutritional issues. Having said that, research suggests that certain foods may play at least some role in affecting symptoms in a small group of people.

In my experience food and monitoring diet has usually been the very first thing that parents will have considered, and in any case monitoring an effective diet is good practice for everybody. In addition I find that families who do carefully monitor diet also become more consistent in monitoring other areas of parenting their child, so a structured diet seems to be a template for structure in other areas of life such as bedtime routines.

The best advice I think is to consult the healthcare professional who you are working with on behalf of your child.

Exercise and ADHD

Exercise is particularly important for children with ADHD. Many children with ADHD with symptoms of hyperactivity and impulsivity may find that exercise can be a positive outlet to release pent-up energy. The truth is that children with ADHD like to move, so organise movement wherever and in whatever way possible. How much, what type and where do you do it are all child, age and stage specific. I would however suggest organising structured movement in terms of an activity or sport rather than allowing them to run off their energy, as issues of hyperactivity and impulsivity can sometimes lead to accidents which can endanger themselves and others.

It may sound unusual, but in my experience some of the martial arts sports work well for children with ADHD, as there is a combination of controlling and supporting your movement in a very structured and respectful way.

Although there is nothing wrong at all in playing football or basketball, if the child does not like these types of sports or has coordination difficulties, martial arts may well be a good alternative.

See the article by Daniel Preiato (2021) in the references for a more in-depth discussion of the issues around exercise and ADHD.

Sleep and ADHD

We all appreciate a good night's sleep, and as we know lack of sleep can affect many things including mood (and we have discussed how important mood is). Unfortunately many children with ADHD have a high risk of sleep problems for a number of reasons. These may include being hard to settle at night, over-activity mentally and physically, being stressed and worried about the next day or perhaps being unhappy or depressed due to difficulties with friendships.

As with nutrition and exercise it will be key to have a structured approach towards supporting effective sleep. This may start with identifying the triggers for difficulties with sleeping and working through reducing the impact of these factors and finding alternative strategies to support effective sleep patterns. There are a number of ways to support effective sleep, from managing screen time through to the potential use of medication. The Sleep Health Foundation is an excellent source of information with regards to this issue so please find their details and some specific tips for children with ADHD in Appendix 3.

And finally

A final point to consider for parents is that new and innovative options are being produced all the time to support children with ADHD.

One example is from a paper published by the Psychiatry and Behavioural Learning Network which outlined how the US Food and Drug Administration has cleared a video game as a prescription treatment for children with ADHD.

KEY POINTS

- Medication can be a sometimes contro-versial but decisive form of action for supporting a child or young adult with ADHD. The crucial issue is being informed and finding a medical prac-titioner who you trust and has good people skills in order to be able to communicate with you and your child.
- There are a range of different medications available and if one does not work (due to any number of reasons) this doesn't mean that another medication won't, so try to be flexible in your thinking if you have decided to go down this route.
- Medication by itself is only one step in the process, and the child will need support in a number of other ways to give the medication a chance of becoming an effective option in sup-porting symptoms.
- It is vitally important to consider options involving nutrition, exercise and sleep hygiene in supporting children and young persons with ADHD.

AND ALSO...

In terms of supporting children with ADHD it is clear that a number of support options are available and should be considered, including medication, to help with learning, behaviour and socialisation. The key I think is to have an open mind in terms of considering the range of options, providing your child with the best opportunity to reach their potential.

Chapter 8

HYPER-FOCUS AND DEVICES

In this chapter we will discuss:

- ◆ what hyper-focus is
- ◆ whether it can be managed
- ◆ screens and their impact.

What is hyper-focus?

As we have already identified, children and teenagers with ADHD can hyper-focus on things that interest them or engage their attention. Increasingly screens seem to dominate the lives of most children and teenagers, and increasingly we parents are bemoaning the role they play in their lives – this can be especially so if your child or teenager's hyper-focus is found in technology. For this reason, we have decided to address hyper-focus and devices within this one chapter.

Hyper-focus often does not come with an element of choice – a certain interest will often seize the individual so that all they want to do is immerse themselves in it.

It can often be painted or described as one of ADHDs superpowers, and it is true that it can be hugely productive if the individual is able to hyper-focus on something useful. However, if the hyper-focus is off task it can be a 'waste' of time, and be seen as a drawback.

Hyper-focus is an intense focus – an individual can do an activity for hours at a time. It can look like detachment but it is normally triggered by an external stimulus, e.g. a computer game or new interest. And it is usually spontaneous and uncontrolled. Hyper-focus can be seen as the opposite of distractibility – which perhaps is why people struggle to understand that it is a feature of ADHD. It comes with an ability to block out everything else going on around the individual.

'Children and adults with ADHD have difficulty shifting attention from one thing to another', says ADHD expert Russell Barkley, PhD. 'If they're doing something they enjoy or find psychologically rewarding, they'll tend to persist in this behaviour after others would normally move on to other things. The brains of people with ADHD are drawn to activities that give instant feedback.'

The benefits of hyper-focus

Hyper-focus can really benefit an individual with ADHD, particularly if the area of intense interest is connected with an area of the curriculum or study, or is considered to be a productive use of time. It can really allow an individual to excel.

However... hyper-focus can also send individuals off down rabbit holes...

The downside of hyper-focus

The less helpful side of hyper-focus can be a loss of sense of time, when the hyper-focus has taken over, meaning that others can find it hard to penetrate and get through, and that the hyper-focus has diverted the individual from the task at hand, and caused them to forget their responsibilities or essential tasks.

Even in the area of academic study hyper-focus can send you off down rabbit holes... For example, a student with ADHD may spend hours making their work pretty, or annotating notes with unnecessary sketches and pictures, convincing themselves that because they are doing 'schoolwork' they are studying, when in fact they are not getting on with the task at hand of revising for a test. When stuck in the zone of hyper-focus it is very easy to lose track of the passage of time and of what is happening in your surroundings.

And of course, if the hyper-focus is on devices, computer games or the internet, then we as parents can find this hugely challenging because it is not seen as 'productive' time. Hyper-focus can also lead to loss of sleep and the knock-on effects, if the individual is unable to switch off.

Some causes of hyper-focus

- Research has linked hyper-focus with low levels of dopamine production, common in people with ADHD, which can make it harder to transition from activities which are high-interest to those which are low-interest.
- We have also highlighted that children with ADHD like instant reward and gratification, and the ability to hyper-focus on something of special interest to that individual can satisfy that need.
- It can also be a coping strategy for some, if they need to block out external stimuli.

Managing hyper-focus

Managing hyper-focus can be tricky when it is in progress – a good idea is to try to agree some limits for when a child or teenager enters this state so that your regulation of it is not unexpected. So, for example, if your child can spend hours on a device as their form of hyper-focus, agree in advance:

- All homework must be done beforehand.
- A time limit will be set.
- That you will give a 'nudge' or gentle tap on the shoulder to rouse them, if they have not managed to self-regulate – and that is their cue or signal to stop. Of course, it is easier to enforce this when there are natural breaks in the hyper-focus activity, so see whether you can weave that in when setting up time limits – for example natural breaks in TV shows, or at the end of an online game, if that is the desired activity.

It is also a good idea to discuss hyper-focus with your child (in calm moments), so that they know that this is part of who they are, but something that they might need a little steering with, to help them manage it. Hopefully, then, they can begin to see your interventions in a more positive light – or at least not overact and become emotionally dysregulated when you need to move them on from an activity.

Dr Edward Hallowell, MD has devised strategies for managing hyper-focus that you can share with you child, or can encourage your teenager to take on board:

1. **Set up external cues to knock yourself out of hyper-focus.** Timers, alarms or phone reminders can alert you to appointments or responsibilities that fade away during a period of hyper-focus.
2. **Discuss how family members, co-workers or friends can help you 'snap out of it' if necessary.** For many, physical touch is a great way to break the spell of hyper-focus.
3. **Set reasonable limits.** Spending three straight days working on an art project might make sense to you, but for the people who love and depend on you, it can be frustrating when you 'disappear'. Decide beforehand how much time you can fairly dedicate to a project, without ignoring your relationships or shirking your responsibilities – and set alarms to ensure you stick to your plans.
4. **Be honest about hyper-focus.** Talk to your friends and family about typical ADHD behaviours and how they manifest for your child. Explain that whilst you are taking steps to help your child harness hyper-focus, they may still be unreachable from time to time. Listen to any concerns they may have, and do your best to mitigate them – but remember that you shouldn't have to apologise for how your child's brain works.

Screens and their impact

One of the reasons we wanted to include screens in this chapter along with hyper-focus is because parents often dismiss the possibility of their child having ADHD because they are able to spend so long on screens. We hope to explain this and demystify it over the next few paragraphs, so that you can see how a dependence or fixation on screens can absolutely go hand in hand with ADHD. We also hope to provide a range of strategies that will help to lead to the personal development that we want to see in our children – and their ability to make suitable choices.

One of the other reasons to include screens in this section is because a lot of us worry about what we perceive to be the excessive and pervasive use of technology – akin to hyper-focus.

Screens tend to have a real draw to children and teenagers with ADHD, because the content is usually fast paced, colourful and stimulating. This makes the use of screens a perfect storm for an ADHD child – especially one that has poor time management skills and may struggle with social-isation. We hope to explain to you that screens can actually be hugely beneficial for ADHD children – but also highly addictive... And somehow as parents we need to be able to navigate through this to create a happy balance for our children. The key to this is to set healthy boundaries that you not only model, but also reinforce and stick to.

The pull of technology for young people is immense and it could be argued that the majority of social interactions for teenagers are now conducted on screens. For ADHD children and teenagers, screens offer a stimulating multi-sensory experience engaging eyes, ears and digits, but in a world where they can cut themselves off from the rest of the day happening around them. Creating and allowing time for them to be in this world can be calming for them – and for you. For some children who find social interactions more challenging, screens can offer them a social world that they have not felt entirely part of during their school day. Screens also allow the child to feel in control of the task that they are performing, and therefore a sense of achievement, self-worth and confidence, in a way that perhaps their school day has not allowed them to feel – screens also give them instant feedback, which satisfies ADHD traits. The key is to help to educate and mentor them, rather than monitoring and enforcing sensible screen choices. One overriding message that really needs to be thoroughly understood by your child is the digital footprint that they create during their screen time – they need to understand that comments and photos can stay online in cyberspace forever. They will also need to be aware of the dangers of providing any personal information, as well as the risks of cyber-bullying and grooming. If they have understood these risks, then you can start to consider how to manage their screen time.

Common problems of screen usage

- Unregulated use of screens means ADHD children can lose their self-control and inhibitory control.
- This leads to less sleep and poor sleep hygiene.
- Schoolwork, homework, sport, exercise and hobbies become marginalised.
- Friendships get pursued online, rather than face to face – these could be inappropriate associations as well as completely harmless ones.
- Digital distraction and burnout.
- Violent online games can lead to aggressive behaviours.
- Online/gaming dependency.
- Isolation.

Common benefits of screen usage

- The internet enables friends to connect across the world and across time zones.
- It allows families to connect across the world and time zones.
- It allows teens to chat and text online, minimising isolation and providing instant gratification.
- Digital tools can be used to become more organised.
- They can help improve some brain activities such as processing speed and working memory.
- They can improve social involvement – especially for socially awkward children who find face-to-face interactions more difficult.
- Screens can help to reduce stress – allowing your child some gaming time (controlled) can help them to de-stress.

TEN TOP TIPS

1. Make sure your child does their homework before their screen time – this will help to overcome procrastination and poor time management issues because they will have completed the night's

essential tasks. However, try not to specifically link the two in a reward or punishment system - it's a simple rule: homework gets done first - no bartering, no blackmail.

2. Shut down the internet at a set time each night and have a rule that all devices are left downstairs - charging if needed - overnight. Ideally that would include the adults in the household too, as healthy screen usage applies to everyone - and we also need to model the behaviour we are trying to enforce.

3. Talk about the pros and cons of the online world with your child; raise awareness of the dangers and help coach them about the downfalls.

4. Set limits and help your child stick to them by focusing on their ability to learn to self-regulate, rather than how bad the games they are playing are, as this will only alienate them.

5. Factor some exercise-based programmes into the screen time use - consider brokering a deal with your child that they need to complete some physical exercise for every half hour/hour that they use their screen - a *quid pro quo*. Or simply have a rule that a set amount of physical activity needs to be done each night (to complement the time they will spend hunched over a screen).

6. If you hear that the use of the screen is causing your child to be dysregulated and angry or frustrated - normally this applies more to gaming than social media - then they need to understand that the rule is that they need to take a break from their screen for a while.

7. Share screen time by watching something with a shared or common interest.

8. Use technology to support education - there are loads of apps to help, for example, Quizlet. Factor in using educational/brain apps - for example a family competition each day to complete Wordle. Use apps that teach mindfulness.

9. Consider whether there is a family 'gaming' game that you can play with your child, so that you have some shared commonality in terms of screen-based conversations.

10. Consider having a rule that there are no video games before

school – they can use some social media if they are completely ready and waiting to leave, but try to resist allowing any form of gaming.

It is worth pointing out that we need to expect some turbulence along the way when navigating screen usage with our child – but especially so in the teenage years. Although very tempting, try not to confiscate devices, but to calmly try to find out what has happened. If for example, your child does gets cyber-bullied there are actions you can take to help manage the situation, by going to the websites your child uses and finding the 'report abuse' or 'block sender' options. You should take screenshots of offensive messages before deleting them in case you need them as evidence in the future. The key in safe screen usage is to encourage your child to talk to you.

AND ALSO...

On a lighter note – the good news is that the ADHD brain appears to respond and engage well with devices and technology, and as our world becomes increasingly digitalised there are likely to be lots of future employment options...in jobs that do not even exist yet.

Chapter 9

THE COLLISION OF HORMONES, ADHD AND THE TEENAGE YEARS

In this chapter we will cover:

- strategies to deal with teenagers' growing autonomy and desire for independence
- establishing good work routines to prepare for public exams
- life beyond education.

Introduction

The teenage years can bring their own set of challenges and highs and lows for young people with ADHD, as well as for their parents and carers. So, we have decided to devote a whole chapter to this particular age and stage of growth and development to try to minimise the bumps in the road that these years inevitably bring.

Children with ADHD during the teenage years have more to deal with and manage than perhaps at any other time of their lives – the onset and progress through puberty coincides with greater academic demand and a heightened desire for independence, all in the context of some executive function development, so that they are having to tackle these years when in fact developmentally they might still be operating and functioning as a pre-teen. The ADHD-effect might mean that you might witness more emotional dysregulation than perhaps you were expecting or that fellow parents experience, and you could be exposed to more impulsivity and volatility, an increased excitability, a low frustration tolerance and a quickness to anger, all of which might add up to a difficulty in balancing emotions – for everyone in the household, not just the teenager!

Despite this – and rather ironically – it is during this period that you could argue an ADHD teenager needs more emotional support and understanding from their support network of parents and teachers.

The teenage years bring with them major new and uncharted milestones and transitions, such as public exams, experimenting with drink (and possibly drugs), learning to drive, experimenting with emotional and sexual relationships, as well as a reassessment of friendships and the forging of new relationships. All this is within the context of teenagers being more hard-wired to thrill-seek and push boundaries in their quest to 'grow up'.

It is also during this period that your family unit and the support you offer your teenager is likely to be challenged and rejected, as your teenager's friends and influences outside of the family begin to take more priority than home.

Throw in surges of hormones, and for some the teenage years can lead to an emotional roller coaster ride.

Because teenagers often need more (but discreet!) emotional support during this period of development, if their behaviours are misinterpreted by home and/or school, triggering reactions of annoyance and frustration in their parents, teachers and carers, the knock-on effect for the teenager can be one of a developing sense of low self-esteem and possibly anxiety... and for some, when left completely unchecked, this could develop into depressive or anxiety-related disorders.

An ADHD teenager's emotional dysregulation and impulsive traits, coupled with increased academic demands, and more nuanced social interactions which a teenager with ADHD might find more complicated to navigate, all add up to days peppered with emotionally fraught social and academic experiences.

In this chapter we will try to help by providing strategies to successfully deal with your teenager's growing autonomy and independence and a desire to be on their own more, and not in the thick of family life. We will try to show how letting teenagers make safe mistakes is a good thing, and how respect for their need for privacy is key to a successful relationship.

The main issues that you will need to be forearmed and forewarned about are:

- An increased influence of peer relations on your teenager.
- Associated with this is a desire for more freedom and independence – within the household as well as outside the family unit.
- An increased desire for independence – which not only affects your teenager's social life, but also impacts schoolwork in the form of increased independent study and homework time.
- Self-organisation skills can also become challenged during this period, as your teenager pulls away from you, and wants to do things 'their way'.
- Thinking about future planning – whether your teenager wants to go to college/university/a training programme/employment.
- Teenagers with ADHD are more prone to risk-taking behaviours for a variety of reasons – impulsivity, inattention, low self-esteem, delayed executive functioning leading to immature thinking.
- For those teenagers on medication, this needs to be considered too.

ADHD gender differences in the teenage years

Much as in the childhood years, your teenager with ADHD will be their own unique self, however there can be some broad gender differences, which may or may not be relevant to the individual that you are parenting:

- As in childhood, a teenage boy with ADHD may be more likely to externalise their behaviours, and therefore be more obvious about their traits. They can be chattier and have fewer controls about butting into conversations and causing interruptions in class. They can also externalise their mood and frustrations, and therefore they can be more physical, and at times more physically aggressive than girls.

- As in childhood, a teenage girl with ADHD may be more likely to internalise their behaviour, and therefore more prone to mask their traits. They can also internalise their mood and appear dreamier and more inattentive. Some will internalise negative moods, which puts them more at risk of low self-esteem and issues such as anxiety and depression. If a teenage girl is prone to aggression, it is far more likely to be verbal aggression as opposed to physical.

Strategies to deal with teenagers' growing autonomy and desire for independence

- Because ADHD brains are routinely emotionally dysregulated, it is good to try to create an atmosphere at home where everyone can laugh at themselves and at mistakes they might make, so that your teenager does not feel that they are the only one! This also enables you to model how to apologise, and how not to take yourself too seriously.
- Do not argue with an ADHD teenager (or child for that matter) in the heat of the moment – they will not be able to think rationally. Tackle it when it has all calmed down, and then explain to them how the outburst made you feel.
- Also take time to cool down yourself if you feel you are about to react, and you feel your pulse increasing – take a time-out and leave the room your teen is in.
- Teens have an increasing desire for independence, and a greater reluctance for support; they therefore need to be encouraged to develop their own strategies.
- Do not always step in to resolve problems – they need to develop independence and self-advocacy skills, but will hopefully still turn to you for bigger issues.
- Focus on positive aspects of ADHD – help your teen to challenge their great energy levels in the right direction: if hyper-focus links in to an aspect of schoolwork, celebrate it; promote creativity traits.

- Use your support network – if your teen is pushing back against you is there someone else that they will engage with within the family unit or outside it who you can call on to help?
- Ask each person in the family to share a high and a low of their day, e.g. two things that were good and one thing that was not.

A special word on developing rapport with teenagers

The consensus seems to be that teens with ADHD have poorer social and communication skills than their peers. This can mean that they are generally less responsive, especially to parents; they can also be more avoidant and more hostile – particularly if you want them to stop doing something that they want to do. This is because they tend to be more compromised in being able to manage their feelings, and they may not possess the necessary skills to handle their growing independence and emotions *yet*! If you remember in Chapter 3 we discussed EF skills and the fact that these continue to mature until a person is well into their twenties. Therefore, these behavioural traits that you might see in your teen reflect the fact that they are not yet fully emotionally mature – but this will come.

The added pressure for teens in dealing with their emotions and their relationships with others is the fear of peer rejection. ADHD teenagers often have 'rejection sensitive dysphoria' (RSD), which will make them even more acutely afraid of rejection. Teenagers who regularly mismanage their relationships and communication skills are more at risk of developing a low sense of self-worth, making them feel demoralised. They can also succumb to a sense of learned helplessness, where they just give up trying to manage their emotions because they cannot get them under control – therefore as parents we always need to be aware of, and monitoring, a teenager's perception of self, and we need to get into the habit of regularly checking that it is still positive and not stealthily becoming negative!

This poses the question – what, as a parent, can we do to help teenagers with how badly they might be feeling about themselves?

- First, we need to work on our child's sense of self. We need to regularly reinforce to them that *everyone* has skills and challenges. We need to help them to recognise their own personal strengths and weaknesses and identify the things that they are less good at and find ways to deal with them, so that they do not feel different

– because feeling different is the worst thing a teenager can feel; teenagers are programmed to want to fit in with their peers!

♦ Try to normalise the way they feel, so that it becomes more of an open conversation within the safety of the walls of the family home.

♦ We need to create an environment where they do not feel awkward and different, and which is open to discussion and to learning.

So, how do we go about creating this? One obvious 'easy win' is to reduce moments of tension and conflict. During a calmer moment when you and your teenager are communicating well, it may be a good idea to discuss with them putting in place an 'amnesty' for when moments of mutual tension arise. This means that it is OK for one of you to walk away from a confrontation, and that the other will understand that the amnesty is being triggered. You can then discuss things more rationally when you are both calmer. It is also worth pointing out that as the adult, you should be more in control of your emotions than your child, and therefore should be a good role model about how to deal with these moments of high tension – however, we all have our breaking points, and in these moments, it is even more important to remember the power of walking away to let the situation calm down.

It is helpful for parents and teens to understand that the struggle is between the teen and their brain because it makes the teen no longer inherently feel like the 'bad guy' – but just that there are times when the ADHD brain takes over. This should help your teenager to understand that their ranges of emotions and their flare-ups are all part of a negotiation between them and their ADHD brain, and the more they understand this the more they will learn how to work with their brains. The teenager also needs to understand that their goals will not always be supported by their brains, because the brain might be looking for high stimulation and production of dopamine – and doing homework or household tasks is not the route to that! Also letting them know you are in it together and together you will get through it is comforting to teens who are always assuming they have done something wrong and at any moment can be rejected for it.

We also need to be aware that when hormones kick in, and when your teenager begins to become more sexually aware, this may feel bewildering, and even at times overwhelming, for your teenager – especially as their executive function maturity might be several years behind their physical maturity. We need to remember this when parenting, as well as remembering that it can be very hard for a teenager to put into words how they feel.

As parents, we can help our teenager manage other aspects of their lives, to try to make life continue to feel as 'normal' as possible, and to help minimise any feelings of being slightly out of control. Therefore, helping to support their organisational difficulties by chunking and breaking tasks down can help to provide a supportive structure within which your teenager can work. For example, if there is an expectation that they clean their bedroom, this can become an easy 'win' and diminish any tension between you if you help them feel a sense of control by:

- Breaking down what needs to be done and chunking it into a written/visual list. It makes it very clear what needs to be done, and the tasks are smaller and more manageable – as opposed to the large and sometimes overwhelming 'you need to tidy your bedroom' refrain.
- It will help to stop procrastination, and also allow them to check things off the list, which is satisfying and makes them want to do more!
- Laminated lists of these more routine aspects of life, that your teenager can use time and again, can diffuse tension, create a sense of 'normalcy' and leave more time and energy for the less mundane aspects of becoming a teenager.

Transitions for teens

Within the context of teens' growing desire for autonomy and independence they will need to have the skills and resources to manage transitions. We already know that transitions (moving from one task to another) can be hard for the ADHD brain; there are three types of transitions to be aware of for teens: physical, mental and emotional.

Physical transitions can be observed by an outsider because they involve movement from one thing to another. Mental transitions take place internally – adjusting or moving from one mental task or thought to another. Emotional transitions are also internal, moving from one emotional state to another, but clearly can be externalised in the form of emotional dysregulation if the transition is not wanted or smooth.

In each of these transitions leaving a task can be hard for an ADHD teenager, particularly if they are engaged or hyper-focusing on it, when it can be particularly hard, or if there is resistance to move to the next task. Teenagers moving into a new task can be prone to distraction or being side-tracked. Some transitions will need understanding and patience in order to help your teen.

To help each type of transition, consider how you can discreetly help:

- Try to help your teen establish routines and set patterns of behaviour.
- Where possible warn your teen about changes/transitions.
- Use checklists and visual reminders.
- Timers and time-based reminders can help.
- Be available to offer emotional support.

Establishing good work routines to prepare for public exams

As we have already established, even though your teen will strive for independence, they still need more support around them than other teenagers their age, because of the impact of ADHD traits and characteristics and the struggles that they might have with aspects of their executive functioning. We have also identified that any support you offer during this period of development you should strive to make more discreet in its nature. Therefore, in the background you should consider keeping a note of all communications from school, and inputting them into a family calendar, so that your teen is reminded without you necessarily needing to intervene and tell them. It is also helpful to try to keep a log of their assignments, homework and deadlines. One strategy is to get your teen to 'buy into' the concept of keeping a visual planner at home where you and your teen note assignments and due dates. Although this means you have full knowledge of school-based deadlines, which your teen may not initially like, it does mean that in the background you are able to provide gentle reminders and keep tags on whether deadlines are slipping or not, which may help to prevent them getting into trouble at school or college.

To avoid unnecessary conflict and opportunities for emotional dysregulation you should encourage your teen to get into the habit of packing their school/college bags the night before – if this level of organisation is a real challenge for them, they should create mnemonics and rhymes to help them to remember essential kit. For the one-off items encourage them to get into the habit of making a note and putting it somewhere prominent to remind them. By developing these self-help skills your teenager will be learning how to become more independent, whilst having self-support strategies.

In terms of helping your teenager to get down to the work itself, consider a routine where your teen works for 15 minutes (depending on their attention span) and then does a preferred activity for 5 minutes (preferably not a video game) and then back to homework.

If their load is heavy encourage them to do the easiest piece first to generate a sense of achievement and motivate them to do more.

Help to break up longer tasks into smaller steps and set deadlines for each step – praise when done.

If your teen goes off task try not to nag them, instead ask them how you can help them.

If working from home proves to be really challenging, consider enquiring (depending on the school or college that your teen attends) whether there is a system which enables students to stay on beyond the school day to finish homework. This may prove to be an environment which provides more structure and fewer distractions and allows your teenager to identify home as a place where they can relax and unwind.

If revision or schoolwork does need to be completed at home – and in reality, because schools close for the holidays, revising for public exams over the Christmas, Easter or Whitsun periods is usually an activity that has to take place at home (or at least not at school) – a place needs to be developed in the home that is distraction-free. Or you can investigate the facilities and opening hours of a local library, if home cannot be a place where regular study can take place.

- Bedrooms are not always the best place to study, because it is a teenager's sanctuary, therefore depending on the rooms available in the house, where possible, the ideal solution is to find a place which is clutter-free and does not have people passing through.
- If this isn't possible, consider the space you have and the resources that are available to help your teenager reduce external distractions – for example noise cancelling earphones can filter out distractions.
- Because the ADHD brain requires a lot of stimulation, it is not uncommon for teenagers with ADHD to want to study with a

distraction happening in the background – such as music playing. The aspect of this to monitor is that the background distraction does not take over, and that the teen is able to study effectively.

♦ Remember that you will still need to factor in movement options, even though your child is now a teenager. Trying to factor in structured movement when studying is still important even if your teenager can't see it that way!

♦ Another important issue is what time of day your teenager studies best – are they more alert and engaged in the morning, or later at night? Set some limits around the time of study if their preference is to study later into the evening – because sleep and a good diet remain as important as ever.

Life beyond education

The teenage years bring new and exciting opportunities with them, but opportunities that may cause parental concern and anxiety – such as your teenager learning to drive, being old enough to get a job (often part-time to fit around education) and having more control over their own sleep hygiene and diet. Good diet, sleep, exercise and good stress management strategies also continue to play a vital role.

Pros and cons of part-time jobs

Jobs can help to foster independence which is (refreshingly) not dependent on academic success or ability; a job can also help to instil some good routines and practices in your teenager. However, if your teen is keen to do some part-time work it will be important to find a job that matches your teenager's strengths and interests, but is also realistic in terms of the time it will take up, especially when balanced with the time your teenager will need to invest in their study and schoolwork – which of course still needs to take priority.

If your teenager does want to earn money but is still involved in education it may be better to do paid work in the holidays, to avoid impacting on the pressures of their academic study.

To help to make this a successful experience, and to help instil good habits and routines for future working opportunities, it may be a good idea if you use IT support to ensure that they are reliable – for example use calendar alerts for shift work or irregular work patterns, or ideally try to help ensure they have the same work pattern each week. Make sure they are punctual by encouraging them to set timers and alarms.

The pros and cons of driving

An ADHD teenager's inattention, impulsivity and distractibility traits can make driving more hazardous for them than it is for their peers because of difficulties staying alert to the road conditions. Increase their awareness of this to try to encourage them to be 'super alert' on the road. For those that are happy to consider it, medication can improve alertness and make them less prone to accidents.

Sleep

One of the biggest things that parents observe in most teenagers is their capacity to sleep late into the day, and one of the biggest things that can impact an ADHD teenager's mood and motivation is their sleep – the quality of it and how long they have managed to sleep for. A lot of ADHD teenagers report that problems with sleep are impacted by racing thoughts.

Try to pay attention to how much sleep your teenager is getting and what their sleep patterns are – and whether they are healthy! Good sleep hygiene will be affected by daytime and evening routines, exercise, diet, exposure to light (melatonin production is important for sleep) and good screen habits. For some teenagers sleep problems will sort themselves out, but if you feel sleep problems are becoming severe or are not resolving themselves, and your teen is getting insufficient sleep – especially on school nights – consider getting further advice. This does not mean that medication is inevitable, because there are a lot of sleep remedies to draw on, but do seek support if you need it.

Co-existing with teenagers

Consider devising house rules in consultation with your teenager – there is a much greater chance that they will buy into them. Focus on a few but important rules, rather than a long list. Consider signing it as if it were a contract. Be clear about your expectations about following the rules – and be consistent!

If rules get broken or your teen commits misdemeanours that you need to pull them up on, keeping your cool is likely to bring about better outcomes – and try to avoid the 'I told you so' or bringing up the past approach.

Ideally consider some typical teen problems that might occur and try to come up with strategies about how you might deal with them, so that you minimise the times you are on the back foot.

Building new and desirable habits

Help your teen to learn new habits:

- Encourage them to choose two things that they are not doing so well. Encourage them to integrate them with tasks which are already automated and successful, e.g. as you are making yourself a coffee also always do...
- Encourage your teen to track their success on a planner or calendar and when they remember to do it encourage a small reward.
- Use rewards to solidify habits, encourage use of sticky notes etc. to set reminders.
- Be patient – your teen will not always get it right, but the more they do it the more they will succeed until it becomes a new habit.
- Use your support network – if your teen is pushing back against you is there someone else who they will engage with within the family unit or outside it that you can call on to help?

Managing friendships and social situations

We need to expose our teenagers to challenging situations and not try to protect them all the time because exposure to tricky scenarios teaches them how to manage different situations and to learn from them.

- Inattentive traits – your teenager may be aloof and reluctant to throw themselves into things. Try to teach them self-advocacy techniques and encourage them to express their emotions. Encourage them to believe that others want to be friends with them.
- Bossiness – try to teach them to be compassionate and flexible. Help your teenager to evaluate their friendships and how they want to be treated by others.
- Try to teach them self-reflection – about themselves and how they treat others.

A word on household chores

Consistency is key and consequences should be meaningful.

Doing chores may help to boost executive function skills – you need to be able to prioritise, plan, remember as well as being able to switch between tasks.

La Trobe University Australia has published an article in *Australian Occupational Therapy* (Tepper, Howell and Bennett, 2022) stating that regular completion of chores is associated with improved academic performance and problem-solving.

Increased potential for risk taking

It is important to note that not all teens with ADHD and impulsive traits will be prone to risk-taking behaviour. You may be one of those lucky parents that does not need to pay close attention to this section of the chapter.

However, for some of us it will be important to be aware of the potential risks that the teenage years bring with respect to risk taking, so that you are aware and forewarned of the signs and primed to spot changes in behaviour which might signify risky decision making is at play.

What can risky behaviour look like?

- **School and college:** In school, a teenager can be more at risk of feeling the force of the school discipline and sanctions policy and even of expulsion because they have the potential to stand out even more than they did when in primary school. Pre-teen schooling tends to permit more movement in class – if you think about the typical primary school class, there tends to be movement around the classroom and shorter tasks because of the developmental age and stage of the children. As we have already learnt, ADHD children are likely to have a developmental delay in their executive functioning, and may well be operating 2–4 years behind their peers. In a secondary school class, this becomes more obvious, meaning poor impulse control, distractibility and inattention – which can manifest itself in behaviours such as losing books and stationery, being late, interrupting and being rude – can result in greater sanctions.

- **Driving:** Inattention and distractibility can lead to more erratic and risky driving. This can manifest itself in behaviours like driving too fast, daydreaming and poor decision making. Teens with ADHD can therefore be more at risk of speeding tickets, parking tickets, accidents and crashes.

- **Alcohol and drugs:** ADHD teenagers can be more at risk of drink and drug experimentation than their peers, exacerbated by their impulsivity. The effects of alcohol and drugs have been said by some to help someone with ADHD to either blot out difficulties that they might be facing at school or socially; others have commented that the use of recreational drugs might be taken by a teen in the belief it will help them with their focus and attention.

- **Sexual activity:** Because a teenager with ADHD can be more wired to thrill-seek, to stimulate the feel-good sensation of dopamine and adrenalin release, they can be more likely to engage in sexual activities earlier than their peers, and/or have more sexual partners. Because of their impulsivity they are less likely to pause and ensure that they are protected by contraception.

What to do if you suspect risky behaviours

- As we have tried to stress throughout this book, one of the most important things is to try to keep the channels of communication open with your teen. The best way to do this is not to react in front of them; try not to get angry or critical – take time out, away from them, to consider any next steps.

- It may be that your teen knows that they are engaging in risky behaviours, and needs help to find ways out – by not over-reacting when you became aware of their changes in behaviour, you will hopefully have kept communication channels open and be able to engage in constructive support and brainstorming about how to stop the risky behaviours.

- Whether or not your teenager is keen for help, or is aware of what they are doing and the risks associated with the behaviour, as their parent you will need to explain the realities to them – and if your relationship means that it is better that the conversation happens with someone else, you will need to consider who is best placed to help your teenager. But it will be important that someone can take on that role, because very often teenagers cannot see the risks for themselves and will need others to help them.

- Try not to turn a blind eye to your fears because you do not know how to deal with them – do not be afraid to seek help from professionals for behaviours that seem too difficult or risky for you to deal with inside the family unit – drug-taking behaviours, for example, may mean that you need to seek support for both you and your teen from experts trained to deal with this.

TEN TOP TIPS

1. Create a structured environment, set house rules, routines and expectations - including monitoring social media use.
2. Be consistent, be clear and be concise; pick your battles and avoid power struggles. Don't take comments personally and react.
3. Understand that anger and frustration are real feelings to those who express them, but have an agreement to walk away until the heat dissipates; always wait to discuss the trigger event/behaviour when things are calmer.
4. Assign a daily household responsibility; discuss with your teenager whether a holiday or weekend job would be right for them depending on their age and stage.
5. Normalise their struggles so they do not feel different from their peers - remind them all teens have emotional swings... And remember your ADHD teen is likely to be socially and emotionally behind their peers - do not expect too much or punish them for it.
6. Be positive, have compassion and do not despair.

7. Do not provide opportunities to argue, and remember, don't take anything personally – it's not about you, it's about them.
8. Reduce the anxiety, don't increase it.
9. Avoid raising your voice, be neutral and speak calmly and remember to think about your body language – keep your hands down by your sides during heightened situations.
10. Celebrate things they are good at to make them feel good about themselves. Celebrate successes and praise good behaviour; when you catch them doing something right, acknowledge it.

AND ALSO...

While there are certainly some increased risks for teens with ADHD as they move through adolescence and into young adulthood, there is no reason why they should not become productive and successful adults. Continued awareness of your teen's specific symptoms and struggles combined with treatment and intervention will help your teen work through the pitfalls to a successful future.

As your child progresses through their teenage years, they are more likely to be able to articulate their own needs and how best to help them - this can help with parenting and ensure that their needs are met within the educational system.

Chapter 10

TRANSITION AND THE FUTURE

In this chapter we will consider:

- transition points and future prospects, as ADHD is a lifelong condition
- how parents and carers may need both the confidence that their child will prosper in the future and the support of professionals and other parents on the journey
- that children with ADHD may need role models to aspire to in their path to adulthood.

Are you worried about, even terrified about the future? Given the right opportunities the future prospects can be a lot better than you might think for your child. The truth is that while schools like compliance, businesses want creativity and people who think differently. This chapter will explore the possibilities and opportunities that ADHD can provide.

Having said that there are hurdles to overcome, particularly in transition from primary to secondary school and secondary school to college or the workplace. Strategies and suggestions will be outlined.

Future prospects

In his ground-breaking talk Changing the Paradigm, the late great educational speaker Ken Robinson (2015) spoke of how schools seek compliance whilst business needs and wants creativity and innovation. His argument was that schools stunt creativity in pursuit of conforming to a common curriculum, and curtail those students who may think and act differently. Obviously we do need to prepare students in the basic skills, but perhaps we are missing some aspects of how we should nurture talent in other areas.

The terms neurodiversity and neurodivergence are starting to be embraced by some schools – and more so business and industry – and ADHD is certainly a learning style that is neurodivergent. Recently within LinkedIn's profiling of skills the term 'dyslexic thinking' was added as a skill under creative thinking. Let's hope that the same philosophy may be attached to ADHD thinking in the future.

In his book *The Global Achievement Gap* Tony Wagner (2009) highlights seven key skills that students need for their future. These were as follows:

1. Critical thinking and problem solving
2. Collaboration across networks and leading by influence
3. Agility and adaptability
4. Initiative and entrepreneurialism
5. Effective oral and written communication
6. Accessing and analysing information
7. Curiosity and imagination.

(Wagner, 2009)

Some but not all of these characteristics describe individuals with ADHD who do tend be non-traditional learners within a school setting, and though they may have difficulties with organisation and planning are often good at problem-solving and lateral thinking.

In addition, in a paper in *Personality and Individual Differences*, Boot, Ericka and Baas specifically focused on the personality strengths of ADHD, listing them as follows:

1. Energetic
2. Spontaneous
3. Creative and inventive
4. Hyper-focused
5. Ability to find unique solutions to difficult problems
6. Adventurous, courageous, thinks 'outside the box'
7. Being able to derive patterns where others see chaos
8. Able to talk about many different topics at one time
9. Constant evolution, continual learning
10. Good in a crisis – some of the most stressful jobs are staffed by those with ADHD
11. Seemingly endless desire to try new ideas, tasks and projects
12. Empathetic and intuitive
13. Entrepreneurial
14. Continual source of new ideas, methods and strategies
15. Ability to see many if not all sides of a situation.

(Boot et al., 2017)

Therefore although ADHD traits may well pose challenges in learning, behaviour and socialisation, they offer individuals who can adapt to address their challenges and develop their strengths fantastic future opportunities. The world needs individuals who think and act differently, as these will be the people who develop new and different products and solutions so that we can constantly evolve to meet our ever changing circumstances.

Transitions

The only certainty in life is change, and as result transitions will usually be of concern especially when moving from primary to secondary school, as children with ADHD can find that transitions can cause anxiety. Key issues that will be important to think about include:

- more freedom and independence
- time management issues
- greater degree of self-organisation
- more independent study and homework
- peer relations
- medication issues
- college/career planning.

In addition the primary to secondary transition may also highlight anxieties in a number of areas including the following:

1. the unknown
2. not liking change
3. more independence in terms of travel
4. the big kids
5. multiple teachers in a large setting
6. many new subjects and a more demanding curriculum.

As a result some of the key factors that would really help children with ADHD to transition successfully would be as follows:

- They belong in their new school, and are well included in school activities and programmes.
- They are positively connected to their peers, other students in the school and to their teachers.
- Their teachers know them, including their strengths, interests and learning needs, and show they are interested in them.
- They are understood and valued as a culturally adaptive or valued person.
- They have an understanding and commitment to their learning pathway through their schooling and beyond.
- Their current learning follows on from their previous learning (the curriculum is connected and continuous) and is appropriately challenging.
- Their learning is interesting, relevant and fun.
- Their families have been included in decisions.
- They are physically and emotionally safe.
- They have opportunities to try new, exciting things and/or extend

their particular skills/interests (e.g. through extra-curricular activities).

Adapted from New Zealand literature on transitions, the Educational Review Office (ERO) identified 12 aspects that indicate students have made successful transitions (Peters, 2010; Kennedy and Cox, 2008).

I believe that the jump from primary to secondary school is absolutely massive, and one of the most important decisions that a parent of a child with ADHD will undertake will be to carefully choose the most suitable secondary school which can offer the level of understanding and support required.

Once again as mentioned in Chapter 6, the choice of school that parents make should be both informed and pragmatic; some of the issues that parents will need to consider are the following:

1. The approach of the school's senior management team towards neurodiversity and ADHD. Does the school practice inclusion (more than just having policies on it) and have staff had training with regards to neurodiversity and neurodivergence?
2. Does the school support rather than penalise the issue of organisation, and will they have a proactive adaptive policy of differentiation for classwork?
3. Does the school have a sensible and informed adaptive plan to support issues of homework for children with ADHD?
4. How will the school plan to support students with ADHD in non-structured time, including assemblies, breaks, lunchtime and field trips?
5. How will and how often will the school communicate with parents, i.e. on a daily, weekly, monthly basis on learning and behaviour issues? Will this be by email, phone, text or face-to-face meetings?
6. What is the school's attitude to potentially working with outside agencies on behalf of the child with ADHD, including what are the arrangements if the child needs to take medication?
7. Who should the parent contact if they have concerns that their child is being bullied by other students at the school or online?

One last tip and probably the most important for parents is not to think that you are lucky to have found a school for your child with ADHD. Think instead that the school is lucky to have your child with ADHD.

In terms of successful transitions to new schools and beyond, this will often depend on a number of factors, but we must mention the word resilience as being especially important.

Resilience

Resilience is a term the Americans sometimes refer to as 'stickability' – a person's ability to persevere with something, or staying power.

To some extent what we are looking for is to help children and young people to become independent and successful young adults, and not be totally dependent on the adults. For them to be able to ride their bike without the stabilisers, as it were. To achieve this, we need to help them develop their resilience.

Resilience appears to involve several related elements:

1. A sense of self-esteem and confidence.
2. A belief in one's own self-efficacy and ability to deal with change and adapt.
3. A repertoire of social problem-solving approaches.

There are a range of factors that can determine innate resilience. The Department for Education (2018) has outlined the key elements of resilience in the child, the family, the community and the school, as follows.

Resilience in the child

- secure early relationships
- being female
- higher intelligence
- easy temperament when an infant
- positive attitude, problem-solving approach
- good communication skills
- planner, belief in control
- humour
- religious faith.

Resilience in the family

- at least one good parent–child relationship
- affection
- clear, firm and consistent discipline
- support for education
- supportive long-term relationship/absence of severe discord.

Resilience in the community

- wider supportive network
- good housing
- high standard of living
- high-morale school with positive policies for behaviour, attitudes and anti-bullying
- opportunities for valued social roles
- range of sport/leisure activities.

Resilience in school

- clear policies on behaviour and bullying
- open-door policy for children to raise problems
- a whole-school approach to promoting good mental health
- positive classroom management
- a sense of belonging
- positive peer influence.

As you see therefore, there are four key areas of resilience to tend to. Although throughout this book we have mentioned a whole host of factors, resilience in these areas is paramount to the long-term success of your child.

Support your own resilience

No one will promote the cause of your child better than you, the parent or carer, but in order to do this you will need to look after yourself. Although every family will be different, in terms of the dynamics that exist between partners, the children and siblings and the extended family members, your mood and protecting your mood will always be absolutely vital if you are to maintain the momentum to support your child, as outlined in Chapter 4.

In terms of looking after yourself – and following the principle of 'it takes a village' to raise a child – I would encourage all parents and carers to join a local support group, or if one does not exist to start one.

I have talked to many parents over the years who have benefitted massively from being able to chat to other parents who are living with a son or daughter with ADHD. A problem shared, they say, is a problem halved – but support groups offer so much more than this. Members will have the best local knowledge of what is available in terms of local services for support and the best options for diagnosis, as well as which are the most proactive schools in the area.

A search on Google should put you in touch with national and local groups (also see Appendix 1 for a list of UK-based groups), but if you can't find a group that meets your needs, start your own. You could recruit members by putting up posters or flyers in schools, the library or church, and at local stores. Talk with ADHD organisations and paediatricians. Be specific about the group's purpose, for example a support group for parents of ADHD children will attract a different membership than one for ADHD spouses.

Although you don't need a professional to run a group, you will need a committed person (or persons) to organise it, as someone will have to schedule meetings and speakers, and perhaps moderate.

While face-to-face support groups are the most powerful way to connect, online groups may work better for you. There are virtual communities supporting every aspect of ADHD.

Finally, another of the positive developments in this area over the last decade has been the growing number of ADHD coaches. I have included below some advice from one Siun Prochazka – Certified ADHD Coach (see Appendix 3 for her details). She suggests the following key issues to think about and discuss with your child.

Equip yourself with knowledge

After the adjustment of the diagnosis sinks in, the most valuable thing you and your child can do is to educate yourself on ADHD. The more knowledge you equip yourselves with, the better the quality of life you will all have as a family. Understanding their own ADHD brain is the most powerful tool your child can have. Being informed about the challenges and equally the strengths that ADHD can bring will go a long way to help your child to understand, accept and appreciate the different abilities that having ADHD can bring them.

Once you have a diagnosis you may be recommended to seek out ADHD coaching or ADHD-specific therapy (the therapist should have a strong foundational knowledge on ADHD) to help your teen navigate this new revelation or to simply understand their ADHD better. Coaching from a certified ADHD coach is an excellent way for your teen and yourself to better understand what is happening inside their brain. When it comes to emotional regulation, meltdowns and arguing can be greatly reduced by understanding how to communicate more effectively.

Understanding the sensitive nature of ADHD

Learning about the ADHD hyper-sensitivity to other people's criticism (even if its intention was to be constructive), judgement or teasing is essential. Rejection sensitive dysphoria (RSD), as it's popularly known on social media, can throw your teenage child off their tracks with sudden emotional outbursts or a rapid retreat into themselves. When a person with ADHD is criticised or teased, even if they just *perceive* criticism or teasing, this can lead to hours of rumination on the interaction where their thoughts are effectively hijacked, bringing their mood down.

As a parent the most important thing to know about RSD is this: whether the criticism was actual or perceived, the emotional impact your child experiences feels the same. Remarks made off the cuff, what feels to one person like fun or gentle teasing, may be taken entirely in the wrong way, sending your child's emotional regulation on a downward spiral.

From my work coaching teenagers and their parents, this is an aspect of ADHD which causes the most breakdowns in communication as well as emotional stress. As RSD can permeate all areas of life, understanding and learning to navigate this with your child is already going to make a big difference in your lives.

At school

Finding out your child's most effective learning modalities – visual, conceptual, kinaesthetic etc. (an ADHD coach will do this with you) – will be key for your child to understand how they can best focus on their schoolwork.

If your child needs movement to learn, for example, then having a quiet way to give themselves that movement in class can be hugely beneficial. This could be squeezing some Blu-Tack between their fingers on one hand while they take notes with the other. Informing the teachers about this will avoid needless confrontations about 'fiddling' in class.

At home

As your child learns more about how their unique wiring works, they will learn hacks that will help them to focus. The neurotransmitter dopamine is essential for focus, and as people with ADHD are unable to produce dopamine at will (Volkow, 2009), it must be consciously encouraged to flow from an external source. The long-held belief of saving your favourite food/activity/experience to last and getting the 'boring stuff' out of the way first does not apply to ADHD. In fact it's the opposite.

Getting that dopamine flowing by doing a favoured activity first will set your child's brain up for paying attention. That's where a 'Dopamenu' comes in handy. This is a list that consists of simple activities that can get your child's interest flowing. Whether that's dancing around to a favourite song, listening to classical music or having the family cat sit on their lap while they study, they will find it easier to transition into the less interesting task when that dopamine is flowing.

If their favoured activity is gaming or something involving screen time, then it's best to have that as motivation for *after* they have done their homework. Transitioning out of screen time into doing their maths homework likely won't be a popular request!

Share

If you suspect you have ADHD yourself, share your challenging experiences and proudly talk about what strengths ADHD has given you. What have these strengths allowed you to achieve? Chances are, your child is coming to terms with feeling different and can't yet see what advantages having ADHD can bring. Strengths like creativity, curiosity, compassion and humour are generally quite pronounced in people with ADHD.

And finally 'ASK THEM WHAT THEY NEED'

Asking your child how you can support them is a powerful way to teach your child to self-advocate. Most of the impact of ADHD is emotional. Because of the everyday intensity of feelings, the tendency to compare ourselves to those around us who seem to manage life a lot better than us, and being hyper sensitive to the actions and moods of others, can erode self-belief.

Give them agency to say what they need. Teach your child to self-advocate by asking them:

- What do you need to help you feel calmer right now?
- What would be the most helpful way for me to support you?
- What is a way I can remind you to study/do chores without it feeling tiresome/restricting etc.?
- What is a way that I can help with things you are struggling with without it feeling like I'm criticising you? How about if I start with what's going well and then ask you how you can bring some of that into what is challenging for you to do?
- I wonder how we can borrow from that enthusiasm and use it to help you start the things you find more boring?
- What I said last night about...seemed to really upset you. What feels like a safer way I can let you know...?
- What does your ADHD brain need right now?

When seeking professional support

Seeking support from a professional who has a superficial knowledge of ADHD may prove fruitless and at best will be a waste of time and money. At worst, they will give misguided support and only contribute to your child's feelings of isolation.

A certified ADHD coach is trained to listen through the ADHD lens. They will hear right away where your child is struggling and be able to explain why it is happening. They will work with your child to build their self-belief and to uncover their ADHD strengths, the ways in which their brains can best focus and how to feel more confident in themselves. They will support your child to strategise ways of using those strengths to help them excel in the areas of life they find challenging. The majority of ADHD coaches have ADHD themselves, which goes a long way to helping clients feel understood and reassures them they are not alone with their ADHD.

ADHD role models

On this note, it is also helpful for children with ADHD to have role models with ADHD to look up to. A host of celebrities, sports stars and successful business people credit their ADHD learning styles as to why they achieved what they achieved.

You can find a list of persons with or rumoured to have ADHD traits in a blog post by Barbour (2020 – see the References).

One of the people on this list is cartoonist and author Dav Pilkey, who told the *Washington Post* he credits his ADHD for his massive success.

Dav is the author of the hugely popular *Captain Underpants* and a number of other children's books, and used to spend his time in classrooms drawing while trying to stay focused on his school lessons.

Fortunately he seems to have had teachers who understood his ADHD traits – although perhaps not all, as some of the teachers he writes about in his books are called 'Miss Directed' and 'Miss Labler', which sounds like not everybody was so understanding.

A final word

There has been an attitude change towards ADHD, from it just being an excuse to it being an explanation; indeed some people argue that it is a gift or even a superpower.

There is nothing wrong in being positive about being different, but I once asked a student with ADHD who was in danger of being excluded from school whether he thought ADHD was a gift – he said, 'Mr O'Regan, if ADHD is a gift then I'm giving it back.'

There is no doubt that ADHD and the different ways that these individuals think and interpret situations can be of major benefit in terms of being able to hyper-focus, creativity and problem-solving, provided they are given the platform to display this talent. For the child and their family, however, it can also be a challenge as well as an opportunity.

The final thought we will leave you with is to remember that ADHD is NOT a deficit and NOT a disorder – it is a developmental difference.

KEY POINTS

- Individuals with ADHD may well find this to be an advantage in terms of future employment as neurodiversity is embraced by business and industry.
- Transition points throughout the school system will be a challenge, as individuals go from primary to secondary and onto college and employment, and key factors need to be considered in all three phases.
- One of the key areas to develop in individuals with ADHD is resilience, of which there are four areas to focus on: the child themselves, the family, the community and the school. Resilience is the key in moving from dependence to independence and achieving 'stickability'.
- For parents who may feel isolated and alone an ADHD support group either online or in person could be a vital lifeline. Here you will meet others who are on a similar journey, and sharing stories, situations, strategies and other pieces of information can be really important. If one does not appear to exist in your area then you can set one up.
- Children need role models to aspire to, and fortunately these days when there is no longer a stigma around ADHD there are a whole host of well-known adults - sports stars, actors and business people - who attribute their success in their field to their ADHD traits. This can only be a good thing for children and young adults to be aware of.
- Remember, ADHD is not a deficit or a disorder - it is a developmental difference.

AND ALSO...

There are those who say that ADHD is a superpower or a gift, and that having traits that allow you to think and react differently gives you an advantage over your peers. There is no doubt that in some circumstances this can be true, but at the same time being neurodivergent - especially as a child - does also create challenges, as well as opportunities for the future. The key I think is to show each individual that you genuinely value them for who they are, and use a personalised approach in supporting them to reach their potential.

References

American Psychiatric Association (APA) (1994) *Diagnostic and Statistical Manual of Mental Disorders* (4th edn; DSM-IV). Washington, DC: American Psychiatric Publishing.

American Psychiatric Association (APA) (2013) *Diagnostic and Statistical Manual of Mental Disorders* (5th edn; DSM-5). Washington, DC: American Psychiatric Publishing.

Attention Deficit Disorder Association (n.d.) 'Top 5 potential benefits of ADHD for employees'. Accessed 7 February 2023 at https://adhdatwork.add.org/potential-benefits-of-having-an-adhd-employee

Barbour, H. (2020) 'Famous people with ADHD'. Ongig. Accessed 7 February 2023 at https://blog.ongig.com/diversity-and-inclusion/famous-people-with-adhd

Barkely, R. (n.d.) Quoted in 'Hyperfocus: The ADHD Phenomenon of Intense Fixation.' *ADDitude Magazine*. Accessed 7 January 2023 at www.additudemag.com/author/royce-flippin/

Boot, N., Ericka, B. and Baas, M. (2017) 'Subclinical symptoms of attention-deficit/hyperactivity disorder (ADHD) are associated with specific creative processes'. *Personality and Individual Differences*, 114(1), 73–81.

Bradley, C. (1937) 'The behavior of children receiving benzedrine'. *Am J Psychiatry*, 94,577–581.

Department for Education (2018) 'Mental health and behaviour in schools'. Accessed 7 February 2023 at https://assets.publishing.service.gov.uk/government/uploads/system/uploads/attachment_data/file/755135/Mental_health_and_behaviour_in_schools_.pdf

Hallowell, E. (n.d.) Quoted in 'The Good, the Bad, and the Ugly of Hyperfocus'. *ADDitude Magazine*.

Hill, P. (2021) *The Parents' Guide to ADHD Medicines*. London: Jessica Kingsley Publishers.

Horvath, J.C. (2016) 'Change your mind about the brain'. *From the Laboratory to the Classroom: Translating Science of Learning for Teachers 1st Edition*.

Krammer, F. and Pollow, H. (1932) 'Uber eine hyperkinetic Erkrankung im Kindesalter'. *Aus der Psychoiatiastrichen und Neuven –Klinik der Charlte in Berlin Mschr Psychiat Neurol*, 82, 21–40.

Mehrabian, A. (1939) *Nonverbal Communication*. Albert Mehrabian at the University of California, Los Angeles, who laid out the concept in his 1971 book Silent Messages.

Miller, L. (2009) *Mood Mapping*: Plot your way to Emotional Health and Happiness. Rodale.

NHS (2021) 'Symptoms: Attention deficit hyperactivity disorder (ADHD)'. Accessed 7 February 2023 at www.nhs.uk/conditions/attention-deficit-hyperactivity-disorder-adhd/symptoms

NICE (2018) 'Attention deficit hyperactivity disorder: diagnosis and management' (NG87). Accessed 7 February 2023 at www.nice.org.uk/guidance/ng87/chapter/Recommendations#medication

Preiato, D. (2021) 'Exploring the link between ADHD and exercise'. Healthline. Accessed 7 February 2023 at www.healthline.com/health/fitness/adhd-and-exercise

Robinson, K. (2015) Changing the Paradigm. Accessed 15 June 2023 at www.ted.com/talks/sir_ken_robinson_changing_education_paradigms. Creative Schools: Revolutionizing Education from the Ground Up. London: Allen Lane.

Still, G. (1902) 'Some abnormal Psychical conditions in Children'. The Goulston Lectures, *The Lancet 1*, 1008–1012.

Tepper, D.L., Howell, T.J. and Bennett, P.C. (2022) 'Executive functions and household chores: Does engagement in chores predict children's cognition?' *Australian Occupational Therapy Journal, 69*(5), 585–598.

Train, A. (1995) *The Bullying Problem*. London: Souvenir Press.

Volkow, N. (2009) 'Identifying brain differences in people with ADHD'. NPR. Accessed 7 February 2023 at www.npr.org/2009/09/11/112752252/identifying-brain-differences-in-people-with-adhd

Wagner, T. (2009) *The Global Achievement Gap*. Boston, MA: Harvard University Press.

Appendix 1: UK-based support groups

National support organisations

ADDers.org
An organisation dedicated to providing ADD/ADHD online information.

www.adders.org

ADDISS
The National Attention Deficit Disorder Information and Support Service.

www.addiss.co.uk

Addup
Addup was set up to bring families together, to guide parents in the right direction to find the practical help they need for their children and to promote both public and professional awareness of ADHD.

www.addup.co.uk

ADHD Foundation
The ADHD Foundation Neurodiversity Charity – an integrated health and education service.

www.adhdfoundation.org.uk

ADHD Voices
ADHD Voices brings the perspectives and experiences of children into international debates around rising child psychiatric diagnoses and the

increasing use of drugs in child psychiatry. These voices contribute to an empirical evidence base that helps to inform ethical debate, clinical judgement and national policy. Voices is a Wellcome Trust-funded research project based at the London School of Economics and Political Science.

www.adhdvoices.com

The Children and Young People's Mental Health Coalition

The Children and Young People's Mental Health Coalition brings together leading charities to campaign jointly on the mental health and wellbeing of children and young people.

www.cypmhc.org.uk

Living with ADHD

This website has been developed to support those who come into contact with ADHD – parents/carers and teachers – and also provides resources for children and teenagers themselves, to help them understand and manage the condition.

www.livingwithadhd.co.uk

Mindroom

A special needs charity for children and adults affected by learning difficulties and learning disabilities.

www.mindroom.org

PATOSS

The professional association of teachers of students with specific learning difficulties.

www.patoss-dyslexia.org

The Royal College of Psychiatrists

The Royal College of Psychiatrists has a policy unit which deals with issues affecting national mental health policy and psychiatric practice. Details can be found on the website (under Policy and Parliamentary).

www.rcpsych.ac.uk/policy

Local support organisations
Baldock/Hitchin/Letchworth/Royston/Stevenage

Angels Support Group – www.angelssupportgroup.org.uk/index.htm

Brighton
ADHD Brighton Support Group – http://adhdbrighton.org.uk

Bristol

Adult ADHD Support Group – http://aadduk.org/help-support/support-groups/bristol-adult-adhd-support-group

Cambridgeshire

Cambridgeshire Adult ADHD Support Group – http://addventure-within.co.uk/support

Chichester

The Hyperactive Children's Support Group – www.hacsg.org.uk/page6.html

Coleraine

Phoenix ADHD Project – www.phoenixadhdproject.org/contact

Dorset

Dorset ADHD Support Group – http://adhddorset.btck.co.uk

Essex

Chelmsford ADHD Support Group – www.adhd-support.org.uk/index.html

Gateshead

Gateshead ADHD Support – www.gatesheadadhdsupport.co.uk/whatis.html

Hampshire

Support group for parents of children with ADHD/ADD and Autism in Farnborough, Hampshire. Runs first Tuesday of every month at the Ship Inn Pub in Farnborough.

Contact: Nikki Roberts – adhdtimeout@outlook.com

www.facebook.com/groups/adhdandASDtimeout

Harrow

Centre for ADHD and Autism Support Harrow – http://adhdandautism.org

Contact: adhd@adhdandautism.org

Hastings

ADHD Support Group Hastings – www.facebook.com/groups/ 1078108339059791

Autism What + Support Group for Autism and ADHD – www.facebook.com/vanessa.lee.1428

Hertfordshire

Understanding ASD and ADHD in Hertfordshire – www.add-vance.org

Lambeth

Lambeth ADHD Support Group – http://turneyschool.co.uk/2018/10/14/lambeth-adhd-support-group-meetings

Lancashire

ADHD Lancashire Support Group – www.adhdlancashire.co.uk

Lincoln

Lincoln ADHD Support Group – http://lincolnadhd.org

Liverpool

Liverpool Adult ADHD (Ladders of Life, LOL) – www.meetup.com/Liverpool-adult-adhd-ladders-of-life-meetup-com

London

London Adult ADHD Support Group – https://sites.google.com/site/joyfivolous/home

Manchester

Manchester Region Attention Deficit Disorder Group – www.maddchester.com

Newcastle

KICK ADHD Support Group – www.netmums.com/newcastle/local/view/support-groups/special-needs-adhd/kick-adhd-support-group-keep-including-challenging-kids

Norfolk

ADD Norfolk – www.addnorfolk.com

Oxfordshire

ADHD Oxfordshire – www.adhdoxfordshire.co.uk/Support-Group.html

Richmond

Richmond ADHD Support Group – www.facebook.com/AdhdRichmond

Scotland

Central Scotland Adult ADHD Support – https://sites.google.com/site/scottishadhdadultsorg/Home

Dundee and Angus Support Group – www.adhddasupport.org

Glasgow Support Group – www.adhdglasgow.org

Stockport

SPACE Stockport – www.spacestockport.org/pages/about.html

West Yorkshire

West Yorkshire ADHD Support Group – www.facebook.com/WestYorkshireAdhdSupportGroup

Appendix 2: Common questions and answers

1. **How do you know if it is ADHD or immaturity?**
   The answer to this question is that you will need a diagnostic assessment to measure a number of factors concerning your child's learning, behavioural and socialisation skills in comparison to developmental norms of children at a similar age and stage of their life.

2. **What does 'executive function deficit' mean in relation to supporting a child with ADHD at school and at home?**
   Children and teens with ADHD are thought to have a developmental delay in their executive function skillset of around 2–4 years, depending on the individual. This means that they will operate emotionally and behaviourally 2–4 years behind their peers.

3. **Do you grow out of ADHD?**
   You don't grow out of ADHD, but hopefully with the appropriate level of support you may adapt towards the more traditional expectations of others while retaining key features that make you who you are.

4. **Why do so many children with ADHD seem to also have ODD?**
   The answer to this question is that it is not the norm for children to have both diagnoses, but the exception. ODD as we have described involves pushback behaviour, and if children with ADHD are not correctly identified and supported it is likely they will display similar signs of frustration. Early identification and targeted support should offset the potential for traits similar to ODD to emerge.

5. **Does ADHD overlap with ASC?**
   The answer is yes, there is a frequent co-occurrence – a number of studies say up to 50 per cent.

6. **How should ADHD be diagnosed and by whom?**
   Usually by a paediatrician, a child or adult psychiatrist, or a clinical psychologist.

7. **Is medication for ADHD dangerous in the short or long term?**
   Medication is prescribed and supervised by an ADHD psychiatrist or prescribing nurse who is trained specifically in this area of the condition. Your GP may agree to work in partnership with them and take over the dispensing of medication; however, the ADHD medical specialist will retain overall supervision. They will conduct a six-monthly medication review. This should ensure that medication levels are always set correctly, and should not be dangerous. If in any doubt, always consult your specialist, and defer to their expertise.

8. **What is the difference between ADHD in boys and girls?**
   The features affect both boys and girls in the same way, but the ratio of diagnosed boys to girls in hyperactive impulsive type is 3:1 (perhaps due to girls masking their symptoms more effectively) and the ratio in inattentive type is 1:1.

9. **Why can children with ADHD concentrate sometimes when they want to?**
   The key is that the child needs to be stimulated by what they are doing or who they are with. So, it's not so much when they want to, but rather when the stimulation is sufficient. Putting it another way, they have a very low threshold for boredom, but can also hyper-focus on something they're engaged with.

10. **Do computers or screens cause ADHD?**
    Digital devices, such as computers and phones, do not cause ADHD. ADHD is a neurological condition. Digital devices may be contributing to the current generation of children perhaps having a desire for 'fast-paced' stimulation, but that is not the same thing as ADHD.

11. **Does diet matter in terms of making symptoms of ADHD worse?**
    Diet can be a factor in exacerbating symptoms of ADHD (think of a sugar rush in a hyperactive child). Conversely, a well-planned diet can help to control some ADHD traits. Therefore, whilst diet

does not directly cause ADHD, a lot of professionals think that a good diet is beneficial and can help to manage some symptoms.

12. **Why do children with ADHD end up in trouble so often?**
Hopefully the chapters in this book have helped to explain why ADHD children appear to get into trouble – but in essence, impulsivity, the need to move (hyperactivity), distractibility and executive functioning delay (often thought to be 2–4 years behind peers), are all contributory factors that can make children and teens with ADHD stand out from their peers, and draw negative attention to themselves.

13. **Will employers ever employ somebody with ADHD?**
Absolutely! ADHD is often seen as an advantage in specific industries and businesses. Also, employers need to adhere to equality, diversity and inclusion regulations in the workplace.

14. **Can you argue that it is the environment at school that is not meeting your child's needs? Can we always meet these needs? Is it OK to say we can't? How is a specialised school for ADHD different?**
To some extent you might say that traditional school settings either are not flexible enough or do not have a philosophy of meeting the needs of non-traditional learners. As a result a specialist school setting that has trained staff in ADHD and has a more creative but structured approach can result in a marked improvement in learning and behaviour outcomes.

15. **What is appropriate discipline for ADHD children?**
Hopefully you have gleaned tips and tricks the whole way through this book about this particular point. However, consistency, clear boundaries, compassion and love are good nouns when thinking about discipline.

16. **Will children with ADHD pass on their ADHD genes to their children?**
The answer to this is that yes this is possible as ADHD does have a high genetic coefficient.

17. **Is ADHD actually a superpower?**
This is a question of perspective, attitude, understanding and support. Although ADHD does provide individuals with many opportunities to succeed in life it may also present challenges. It is common for many successful and brilliant people to have

difficulties in organisation, planning and other features highlighted in this book. Recognise the strengths and support areas of need.

18. **Is it possible that my partner or I might have ADHD?**

Based on the answer to question 16, yes this is possible. Many parents after finding out that their child has ADHD get themselves tested and find that they have the condition too.

19. **Are there other families out there who are going through what we are going through and how could we get in contact with them?**

Absolutely! Some regional organisations and groups have been signposted in Appendix 1, however, a search of the internet for specialist groups in your area will also probably yield plenty of results.

20. **How do to broach this topic of ADHD with grandparents for the first time who are not ready or open to a discussion about their grandchild showing clear tendencies and what is your view on whether it should be left until it is felt they are ready or good ways to introduce the idea?**

This is a common question amongst parents – actually in my experience grandparents are more informed than you might think. Being experienced parents themselves they do notice developmental differences in children. Maybe the answer is to gradually introduce the idea that the school have mentioned that there is something different to how your child reacts in comparison with their peers. As a result you are going to investigate what this might be. They won't always agree that ADHD is the cause, but they can't argue with this approach.

Appendix 3: Resources on ADHD

To further increase your understanding of ADHD and associated conditions in terms of impact and intervention some suggested resources would be as follows:

www.additudemag.com

https://chadd.org

www.youtube.com/@HowtoADHD

www.adhdfoundation.org.uk

www.additudemag.com/adhd-symptoms-test-children – An online child ADHD screener tool; one of many, so do take a look at what else is on offer online.

www.additudemag.com/neuroqueer-adhd-lgbtq – Article on LGBTQ+ and ADHD with further links to related articles.

https://addca.com/adhd-coach-directory – Find a certified ADHD coach or family ADHD coach.

www.uniquelywiredcoaching.com – Siun Prochazka, Certified ADHD Coach, @uniquely_wired_adhdcoach

www.sleephealthfoundation.org.au/pdfs/ADHD.pdf – The Sleep Health Foundation is an excellent source of information on sleep health; this link has some specific tips for children with ADHD.

www.eunetworkadultadhd.com – The European Network Adult ADHD is an organisation founded in 2003 that aims to unite clinicians and researchers from across Europe working with adults with ADHD. Currently, there are 24 countries and 74 professionals involved in this network. The aims of the European Network Adult ADHD are (1) to increase awareness that ADHD is a lifelong condition; (2) improve diagnostic assessment and treatment; (3) support and facilitate international research; (4) improve access to services; and (5) establish cooperation between professionals involved in child and adult ADHD.

www.lifecoach-directory.org.uk/articles/adhd-coaching.html – Life Coach Directory was set up to increase the awareness of life coaching and enable visitors to find the most suitable coach. Coaching is the process of guiding a person from where they are, to where they want to be. Only life coaches who have shown proof of qualifications and insurance cover, or proof of membership with a professional body, are listed. This URL is the page dedicated to ADHD coaches.

www.ukaan.com – The UK Adult ADHD Network (UKAAN) was established in response to UK guidelines from the National Institute of Health and Clinical Excellence and the British Association of Psychopharmacology who for the first time gave evidence-based guidance on the need to diagnose and treat ADHD in adults as well as in children; and in response to the relative lack of training and support in this area for professionals working within adult mental health services.

Instagram/TikTok

@howtoadhd

@cobywattsmusic

@connor.dewolfe

@additudemag

@dt.perry

@uniquely_wired_adhdcoach

@internalconnections

Index